Cookery School

Fish

Cookery School
Fish

Getting the best from your main ingredient

Joanna Farrow

NEW
HOLLAND

Contents

Introduction

Beautifully fresh fish is often best served simply cooked. A whole grilled (broiled) plaice topped with a dot of butter and seasoning; a plump baked salmon fillet drizzled with a squeeze of lemon; or mackerel fried with crispy bacon – all delicious dishes that tempt the palate with their sublime flavours and divine taste. These dishes are simplicity itself to cook, and may help demystify cooking with this ingredient. Most of us are more wary of cooking fish than meat, perhaps because we're simply less familiar with it. Sure, fish does require more careful treatment than meat, as it's so quick to cook through and may fall apart if overdone. Like other ingredients it will also dry out if cooked for too long, and then of course, there are the bones – perhaps the reason why most people shy away from cooking and eating this versatile ingredient.

There are many different ways of cooking fish, and each chapter of this book provides easy-to-follow instructions for each method, as well as plenty of recipes to try with your newly honed skills. From grilling and barbecuing to roasting and poaching, simple recipes are provided to illustrate the process. So, even if you've never cooked fish before, you'll see just how straightforward it is. Many of the recipes can be prepared and cooked in less than 30 minutes, which makes fish the ultimate fast food!

SUSTAINABLE FISHING

In recent years issues such as sustainable fishing and responsible buying have become very focal to the fishing industry and our shopping habits. Sustainable fishing and protecting the marine environment will help to ensure that we can enjoy a wide range of seafood, both now and into the future so it's worth using our 'purchasing power' as an influence.

The way in which some fish are caught can have an impact on other types of fish in the same waters so it's important that you choose fish with the fishing method clearly labelled. This might be using hooks and lines, nets and pots, or even in the case of scallops and clams, harvesting by divers – a good fishmonger will be able to advise you and supermarkets should label their products accordingly. Products should be avoided if they are fished by bottom trawling, a method of fishing in which a net the size of a ruby pitch is dragged along the bottom of the sea floor, churning up and destroying the environment as it goes, and capturing unwanted species. Pair netting, in which two boats run alongside each other with a net between the two, also causes 'bycatch', meaning species that are not wanted for sale are caught in the net, and are then thrown back overboard, but generally when they are dead. Bycatch includes all manner of sea creatures, as well as fish not included in the quota. Generally, there has been a lot of progress in this area but there's still much further to go. You can check out various marine conservation and sustainable fishing websites for information on responsible fishing and purchasing. You'll also find lists of fish that we should be eating less of due todepleted stocks, as well as those we should be making every effort to enjoy more of. There are also the fish 'in the middle', those that should be eaten occasionally – maybe a treat to enjoy once in a while!

There are literally dozens of types of fish to try! We may be unfamiliar with many of these, or unsure what to do with them, but many are becoming more commonly available. Now is the time to experiment with the unfamiliar – they just might become your everyday favourites.

If you can, choose locally caught fish in favour of those that might have been flown a long distance. This also makes us more aware of fish 'seasons' as some types of fish, like other foods, have seasons and are only available at certain times of the year. Some types of fish, like other foods, have seasons and are only available at certain times of the year.

Farming fish

This rapidly expanding worldwide industry can offer a sustainable alternative to over-fished wild stocks as well as cope with the increasing demand for popular species. Many are now farmed including salmon, trout, tilapia, sea bass, halibut, turbot, cod, sea bream, tuna, mussels, clams, oysters and prawns. Fish farming has suffered bad press on various aspects of its production including its use of chemicals, wild feed, lack of space, pollution and taste. Ongoing research and new techniques are working to 'clean up' fish farming to make it a worthy alternative to buying wild fish.

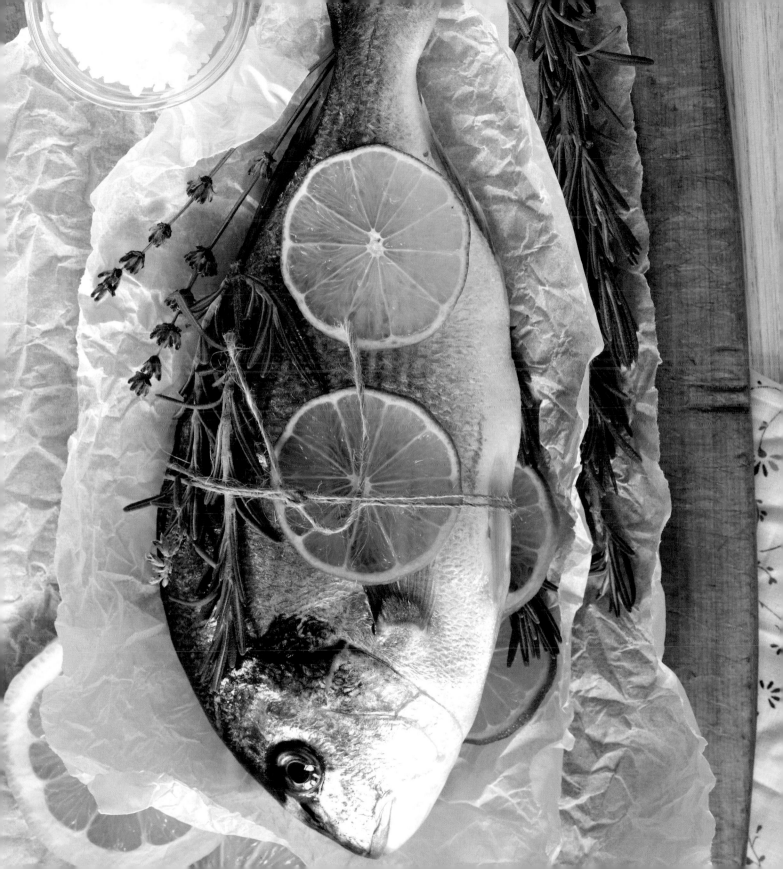

BUYING FISH

Fresh fish

Choosing quality fish is the first step to creating a beautifully cooked dish, so it's worth being very selective. If you're lucky enough to have a good fishmonger near you, and the quality and source of the produce is guaranteed, then you're part way to producing a delicious dish. When buying fish it pays to be flexible about the type that you buy – the fish you want might not be available on that particular day, or you might see another variety that looks more appealing. The fishmonger will be able to advise you on substituting one fish for another, as well as on fish flavours and textures, how much you'll need to buy and cooking methods (for when you confidently deviate from the recipes in this book!). Most importantly the fishmonger should know where and how the fish has been caught. The fish shop, or counter, should not have a strong, stale fish smell, but subtle fresh sea salt aroma. Avoid any fish, or fish counters, with a strong ammonia smell.

Choose whole fish with bright, plump eyes, rather than sunken dried ones. They should have a glossy, fresh sheen and an air of slipperiness about them – as though they've only just been caught. The bodies should be plump and firm with bellies intact rather than split, which might be an indication of staleness, particularly on oily fish. Fillets should look moist and succulent with flesh that holds together firmly. Avoid dull, ragged, dry looking pieces. Oily fish like mackerel, sardines and herrings deteriorate quickly so be particularly careful when choosing these.

Frozen fish

Today's fishing vessels are fully equipped with freezers, meaning that many fresh fish caught at sea will be prepared for sale and frozen while still at sea, so it's fished and frozen within a short time span.

White fish and shellfish are good products to buy frozen, but always make your purchase from a store with a fast turnover of stock. The flavour of fish will gradually deteriorate if it is frozen for more than six months. Fish such as salmon and trout will keep for up to three months in the freezer, but some oily fish should never be frozen.

When looking at fish that has been frozen, you need to check it in much the same way as you would fresh fish. Flesh that is browning, looks flaky or dry has probably been stored too long or incorrectly and should be avoided.

Shellfish

These fall into two groups, crustaceans and molluscs. Crustaceans include prawns, shrimps, langoustines, crab and lobster of which the latter two can be bought live as well as cooked. For the novice it's best to buy cooked crab and lobster and extract the meat from them following the methods in the preparation techniques section. Raw prawns are now widely available and are so easy to fry, bake, grill or barbecue. Warm water prawns, including king and tiger prawns, may be 15–20 cm (6–8 in) long, though generally they're smaller. These are usually the ones we buy raw, whereas cold-water prawns are bought ready-cooked. Cooking raw prawns couldn't be easier, they're ready when they turn from a bluish-grey colour to coral pink.

Molluscs are invertebrates and can be divided into three groups. Single-shelled molluscs (gastropods) include winkles, limpets and whelks, while hinged-shell molluscs (bivalves) include mussels, oysters, clams, cockles and scallops. These are the most popular of the molluscs and are best bought live for cooking at home. You'll sometimes see ready-cooked bivalve molluscs packed in vinegar or brine. These are acceptable for adding to pies, sandwiches and pasta dishes but for the best flavour buy live ones and cook them yourself. It's easy – and such a treat.

Cephalopods, the third group of molluscs, have no shells but soft bodies and tentacles. Squid, cuttlefish and octopus are all delicious. Squid is the easiest to deal with (see preparation techniques) and is used in several recipes in this book.

Most shellfish have seasons though some such as mussels, scallops and oysters are cultivated to produce year-round supplies. It's harder to judge the freshness of shellfish than it is for other types of fish. If you have a good supplier of regular fish the chances are that the shellfish will be of equally good quality. There are various things to look out for. Shellfish should smell sweet, fresh and of the sea. The shells should be moist and glistening rather than dry. Whole prawns, crabs and lobsters should be completely intact without missing heads, tails, legs and pincers. Most prawns we buy have already been frozen. Those displayed on the counter, either raw or cooked, have also very likely been frozen. It's worth asking for prawns that are still frozen as you won't know how long the defrosted ones have been on the slab. If buying shell-on prawns, allow double the weight you'd need for shelled prawns.

The shells of mussels, clams, cockles and oysters should be tightly shut. Any open shells should close when tapped. This is, of course, difficult to do when you're standing at the fish counter so cast your eye over the whole batch. A tray of gaping, gasping bivalves is an indication that they're past their best. Scallops are usually bought ready shelled. These should look plump, pale and juicy, not shrivelled and wrinkly. Occasionally you'll see scallops sold in their shells, or half shells. These are the only bivalves that don't need to be live for cooking.

STORING FISH

Fish flesh is soft and delicate and used to cool or very cold water. As soon as it leaves this environment it starts to spoil. Commercial fishing boats, which might be out at sea for a week, have the facility to store fish on ice at a temperature of around 0°C (32°F) which keeps the fish from spoiling. Most domestic refrigerators are set at 1–5°C (34–41°F) so fish will deteriorate more quickly at this slightly higher temperature. For this reason, it's best to cook fresh fish as soon as possible, preferably within a day of buying it. Fish should be stored in the coldest part of the refrigerator. (It's worth buying a refrigerator thermometer to assess which area is coldest.) Arrange whole fish or fillets flat on a plate, or lipped tray, so any juices don't drip onto other foods. Cover loosely with a damp cloth or cling film (plastic wrap). If you've bought whole fish, gut them as soon as it's convenient as this part of the fish spoils first. A fishmonger will do this for you. However, techniques such as cleaning, scaling, boning, filleting and shelling seafood are skills that are easy to learn. It's both satisfying and rewarding to know how to do them. You'll find all the basic skills included in the book. Smoked fish should be sealed in a bag so its smokiness doesn't permeate other foods.

Storing shellfish

Shellfish are best eaten as fresh as possible although some very fresh shellfish will keep in the refrigerator for a couple of days before eating. Unwrap and place on a plate or in a bowl and cover loosely with a dampened cloth so the shellfish can breathe but stay moist. A dishtowel that you've wet and wrung out is ideal. Store in the lower part of the refrigerator or salad drawer until ready to cook. Don't submerge live mussels, cockles or clams in water. Store oysters and scallops with the rounded shell face down so the juices don't escape. Whole squid can be prepared, and stored in the refrigerator for a couple of days. Squid and raw or cooked prawns, whole or peeled, also freeze well, as long as they haven't already been frozen.

Freezing fish

Much of the fish that is sold in supermarkets is frozen. Freezing causes minimal damage to the structure of fish flesh provided it's done properly. In fact, it's better to buy frozen fish for your cooking rather than fresh fish that is of dubious quality.

If you're freezing fish that you've bought fresh, scale and gut it first if bought whole. Thoroughly dry fish on kitchen paper as water expands on freezing and will damage the texture of the fish. Wrap well in freezer bags, eliminating as much air as possible and label before freezing. You might know what you're putting in the freezer but you might not remember what it is three months later. White fish and smoked white fish freeze better than oily. Thaw fish overnight in the refrigerator, or using a microwave.

PREPARATION TECHNIQUES

This chapter covers all the preparation techniques for fish and shellfish prior to cooking so that you can see how easy it is to master such skills as filleting, boning or skinning a fish. Like most techniques you might find that you work slowly at first (and that your attempts might be a little ragged), but all are achievable with just a little practice and a few decent tools. A good fishmonger will do all the preparation for you of course, but it's better to do it yourself, or at least know how to do it should the occasion arise when you're presented with a whole, freshly caught specimen. Don't forget to keep all the trimmings and bones for homemade stock, see basic recipes.

Fish can be divided into two main groups, round and flat, and within these groups the preparation techniques are very similar regardless of fish type. Preparation usually depends on the way in which the fish is going to be cooked so refer to your chosen recipe before you start.

Trimming fins

Some round fish have incredibly spiky fins that can be removed before cooking, if you prefer.

Use sturdy kitchen scissors and simply cut away the fins, keeping the scissors as close to the body as you can.

Work from the tail to the head end for best results.

Scaling

Fish scales vary in size from coarse, brittle ones present on fish like snapper and sea bass, to the softer, smaller ones on flat fish. The texture of scales is unpleasant to eat so are best removed before cooking, particularly if you intend to eat the skin. They also spoil the appearance of the fish. If you can't see any visible scales on the fish and want to check whether the fish needs scaling or that the fishmonger hasn't done it already, run a knife from the tail end upward to see whether it lifts any scales. Scaling is a messy job as they

tend to fly in all directions as you remove them, and are difficult to track down on kitchen work surfaces because they are translucent. To overcome this, put the fish in the sink and just cover with cold water as you work or tuck the fish into a plastic bag to catch the scales. Work from the tail towards the head by running a fish scaler or the back of a knife from the tail toward the head end. Turn the fish and repeat on the other side before rinsing the fish under cold running water. A few fish such as mackerel, herrings and lemon sole do not need scaling.

Removing gills from a round fish

However you're cooking your fish, removing the gills isn't an essential procedure though they do have a bitter flavour that can taint the rest of the fish, particularly if it's poached. They also filter impurities and (like the guts) are quick to deteriorate once the fish is dead. For this reason they're often removed before

cooking. Lift the gill flap (the hard, rounded section at the side of the head that looks like a giant scale) and cut out the gills with scissors. Repeat on the other side of the head. On smaller fish such as mackerel, sardines and herrings you might find it easier to pull out the gills through the gutted stomach cavity.

Gutting a whole round fish

Some fish, usually flat fish, are gutted before you buy them. If you buy whole fish, gut it (or them) as soon as you get home because this is the part of the fish that spoils first.

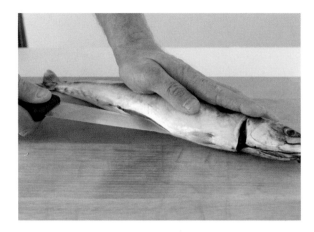

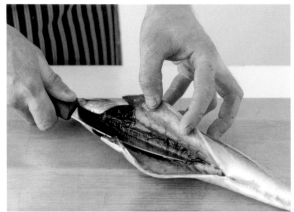

Arrange the fish on a board and press the belly down flat with one hand. (Gutting is a messy job so you might want to cover the board with newspaper or a bag before you start.) Push the tip of a knife into the belly and work towards the vent and then head end of the fish.

Scrape out the contents of the cavity and any areas of blood clinging under the backbone using the tip of the knife. Rinse the fish under cold running water.

Scoring round fish

Scoring a whole fish helps speed up cooking and allows seasonings, marinades or rubs to penetrate the flesh. Using a sharp knife make deep diagonal cuts into the flesh, making the cuts about 2–4 cm (¾–1½ in) apart depending on the size of the fish.

Skinning fish fillets

The dark skin side of flat fish was once considered inferior to the white side and dark skin fillets were even cheaper to buy. Now that crispy fried fish skin is popular we'd never consider it inferior though there are some recipes that are best using skinned fillets. Use this easy technique for both round and flat fish fillets.

Place the fillet, skin side down, on the board and grip the tail end firmly with one hand. Slip a large or filleting knife between the flesh and skin at the tail end. Use a sawing action as you work towards the thick end of the fillet. By pulling at the skin with your free hand you'll make it easier for the knife to work between skin and flesh.

It sometimes helps to rub your fingers with a little salt before gripping the end of the skin as it can be a bit slippery.

Removing pin bones

Pin bones are the stray bones that are often found in fish fillets. They're always found at the thick end of the fillet where it was once attached to the rib area. These are easy to remove using ordinary tweezers or better still, fish tweezers specifically designed for the job.

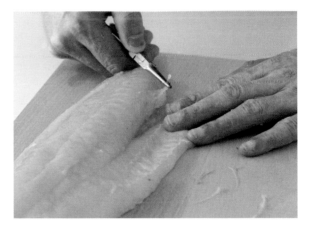

Feel along the fillet with your fingers to locate the bones. Grasp the top of the bone with the tweezers and pull away quickly.

Skinning Dover sole

The dark skin side of Dover sole has a more leathery texture than lemon sole or plaice. Because the flesh is considered such a treat the skin is often removed before cooking. Although not a technique cook's use frequently, it's a good skill to add to your repertoire.

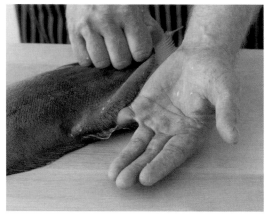

Make a shallow cut across the skin, just above the tail. Push the knife in between the skin and flesh until you've a little pocket that you can push your finger into.

Work your finger between the skin and flesh until you've released an area of skin that's large enough to get a grip on.

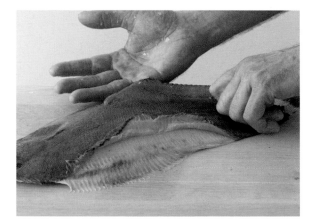

Salt the fingers of both hands. Hold the tail with one and the released skin with the other. Give the skin a sharp tug so it comes away in one piece.

If the skin starts to pull the flesh away with it, use the tip of a knife to release the skin and try again.

Boning small whole fish

This technique is easier than it looks, and is great for removing all the bones from small fish such as herrings, sardines and small mackerel. Serving them like this is sensible for those who don't like fiddling with bones.

Cut the heads off the gutted fish and place the fish skinside uppermost on a board, opening out the underside so the fish sits as flat as possible. Press down firmly along the backbone with the thumb or heel of the hand, depending on the size of the fish. You'll feel the bone being released from the flesh. Turn the fish over. Grip the end of the backbone and pull it away from the flesh, using your other hand to remove any bits of flesh that are clinging to the bone. Cut off the bone and tail end using kitchen scissors, or, if you want the tail attached for presentation, snip off the backbone just above the tail.

Boning monkfish

Monkfish is always sold skinned and often filleted. If you buy fillets, particularly smaller ones with the central bone still intact, it's very easy to remove.

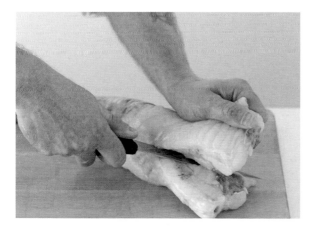

Feel along the thick end of the central bone with your fingers to locate it. Slip the tip of a knife down one side of the bone working from the head to tail end, cutting right through the fillet so it can be completely removed.

Repeat on the other side. Any dark mottled areas of membrane should also be removed by sliding a knife between it and the firm white flesh.

Stuffing fillets

Stuffing fish is one of the easiest and most appetising ways to add flavour. The simplest way is to simply tuck well-flavoured ingredients like lemon or lime slices, herb sprigs, garlic cloves or sliced shallots into the cleaned cavity of a large whole fish or individual fishes before cooking.

You can also stuff small fillets such as plaice or mackerel by spreading a loose stuffing along the fillet and rolling it up, (see Serrano-wrapped roasted monkfish) or sandwiching two plump fillets with filling and tying at intervals with string (see roasted fish with chorizo stuffing). These are both good ways of making fish portions go a little further. Stuffings can include breadcrumbs to add volume but make sure the stuffing includes intensely flavoured ingredients that'll permeate the fish. Once the stuffing is prepared and cooled (if cooked), check over the fish for any stray bones and remove the skin if the recipe requires.

Rolled stuffed fillets

Spread the stuffing down the length of the fillets, roll up the fillets starting at the thin end so the thickest area of meat cooks through quickly. Hold the rolled fillets in place with wooden toothpicks.

Sandwiched fillets

Use even-sized fillets and sandwich them with an even thickness of stuffing. Spread the stuffing along one fillet and position the second fillet on top. Strips of bacon, Prosciutto or Serrano ham can be wrapped around the fillets before tying them at 5 cm (2 in) intervals with string. Transfer to a greased roasting pan, ready for cooking.

Using fish cutlets

Fish cutlets are usually 3–4 cm (1¼–1¾ in) thick and are the slices cut from a large whole round fish such as salmon, grey mullet and large sea bass. Those cut from the rear of the fish are solid (sometimes known as steaks) while those cut from the front are more crescent shaped due to the fish cavity. Because of the backbone and rib bones (on cutlets taken from the front of the fish), cutlets are generally a less popular choice for cooking than fillets and are not as widely available. They can easily be used instead of fillets in most recipes but will take slightly longer to cook.

How to fillet a round fish

This technique is used for round fish of any size including salmon, sea bass, trout, mullet and mackerel. These have a firm backbone along their upper bodies, which is easy to slice the flesh away from, and curved rib bones underneath. This is the trickiest area to remove the flesh from as the bones are spindly and the fillet is thinner. You might well cut through some of the small rib bones but these can be easily removed after filleting, see Removing Pin Bones.

After scaling and gutting, cut off the head by making a diagonal cut so you don't waste any meat from the back of the head. If you find it hard to cut though the backbone of a larger fish, position the thick end of the knife over the bone and tap the top of the knife firmly with the end of a rolling pin or mallet.

Using a filleting knife held horizontally, cut into the flesh at the head end, keeping the knife as close to the backbone to avoid wasting meat. Continue to slice away the flesh at the head end, keeping the knife as close to the backbone to avoid wasting meat.

Continue to slice away the flesh from the bone, working down toward the tail end.

Holding the released part of the fillet with one hand, use short cutting strokes to release the flesh from around the rib.

Turn the fish over and fillet the other side in the same way. Skin the fillets, if required and check for small bones.

How to fillet a flat fish

Flat fish such as Dover or lemon sole, small brill and large plaice can be cut into two large fillets or four smaller ones. The trick is to keep the knife running against the flat bones so you don't waste any of the meat. Keep all the bones for a really good stock. You'll find that the fillets on the dark side of the fish are slightly plumper than the white.

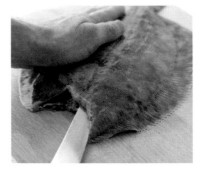

Position the fish, dark skinned side uppermost. Insert the tip of the knife into the fillet just above the bone. Keeping the knife horizontal against the backbone.

Keeping the back of the knife close to the backbone, push the knife forwards and use a sawing action to release the fillet from the bone.

Release the fillet at the tail end. Lift away the fillet to reveal the backbone. Use a gentle stroking action to release the fillet around the backbone, holding the released fillet away so you can see where you need to cut.

Continue to release the fillet away from the other side of the fillet.

Work toward the thin edges of the fish until you're able to release the fillet completely. Turn the fish over and use the same technique on the other side. The fillets can be skinned and cut up.

Preparing mussels, cockles and clams

Prepare these bivalves up to a few hours before serving, rather than when you get them home. Wild mussels might have scratchier shells and more barnacles attached to them than the rope-grown farmed mussels. You can scrape the barnacles off with a knife so the shells look more attractive. Mussels also need de-bearding. These are the dark, tough fibres that they use to cling to ropes or rocks. Simply tug them away with your fingers.

Wash mussels, clams and cockles in several changes of cold water to remove any grit and sand. As you drain them, discard any damaged shells or any open ones that don't close when tapped firmly on the edge of the sink.

Shelling prawns

Raw and cooked prawns are shelled in the same way. Remember to keep the heads, shells and tails for making stock.

To remove the heads, pinch your finger and thumb together at the point where the head meets the body and twist away the head. Pinch off the tails and then peel away the shells.

De-veining prawns

The black vein that you might see running down the length of a large raw prawn is the digestive tract. Removing it is not essential though it can look unsightly. To remove, make a shallow cut along the peeled prawn over the black line and pull out the thread. It'll come away very easily.

Opening scallops

Unlike other bivalves you can shell scallops as soon as you get them home, then refrigerate them until you're ready to cook them, ideally within 24 hours. The white fleshy part of the scallop that we eat is the strong muscle that holds the two shells together and it's this that needs to be sliced through to open the shell.

Hold the scallop with the flat shell uppermost and push the tip of a sturdy knife or oyster knife between the shells and lever them apart. Slide the knife against the flat top shell and sever the muscle from it. At this point the two shells will come apart easily. Cut the scallop away from the rounded shell taking care not to cut into the muscle meat. Pull away and discard all the parts of the scallop that are not white muscle or coral. Rinse if necessary and pat dry on kitchen paper. Store on a plate, loosely covered with a damp cloth.

Opening oysters

These are the most difficult of the bivalves to open as the shells are sturdy and thick. It can feel like you're trying to lever open a rock. With practice the task gets easier although there are always a few oysters that remain stubbornly shut! It's safest to use a proper oyster knife, which are available from good kitchenware stores. Protect the hand that's holding the oyster with a folded dish towel of several thicknesses, or an oven glove. Line a tray with crumpled foil or ice cubes so the oysters, still in their rounded shells, can be supported without losing all the precious juices.

Hold the oyster with the flat shell uppermost. Push the tip of the knife in between the two shells, just to one side of the hinged end until you can feel that the tip of the knife is firmly lodged. Using plenty of force, twist the knife to lever the shells apart. Slide the knife against the flat top shell to release it completely. Discard the top shell and run the knife under the meat in the lower shell to release it, but leave in the shell along with the juices.

How to remove meat from a cooked lobster

Cooked lobsters are easier to deal with than crabs as there are fewer nooks and crannies to scoop the meat out from. Most of the meat in a lobster is taken from the claws and tail. This can be added to salads and other dishes or returned to the shell for serving with a bowl of mayonnaise, garlic or saffron mayonnaise (see basic recipes), lemon wedges and bread for a simple treat at lunch or supper. Cut into chunky pieces, lobster can also make an exotic alternative to prawns in a fresh, summery salad. Twist off the claws and legs from the lobster and reserve.

Arrange the lobster out flat on a chopping board with the tail extended. Push the tip of a large sharp knife down through the top of the head and bring it down vertically to slice the head in half. Turn the lobster round and slice through the tail to divide the lobster in half.

Use the tip of a knife to lift out the dark coloured, thread-like vein that runs down the length of the tail. This is the digestive tract. At the head end of the lobster, pull out the small stomach sac, which lies behind the mouth and small grey gills. These are the only inedible parts.

The 'tomalley' is a pink or greyish soft meat in the centre of the body. There might also be a grainier textured 'coral', which is pink or deep red in colour. Both these are edible and delicious.

To serve the lobster in its shell, lift out the white tail meat and twist it free at the body end. Cut into bite-sized pieces and return to the shell. Crack the claws with a hammer or lobster crackers to open them so the meat is accessible. Do the same with the legs if they are large. Serve with skewers for scooping out the claw and leg meat. (Even if they're too small to scoop out the meat you can still suck out the juices, so you don't waste any of it's delicious flavour.)

How to remove meat from a cooked crab

Choose a cooked crab that feels weighty and remove the meat from it on the day you buy. If you're preparing a recipe in which white and brown meat are used separately, collect them in separate bowls. You can also pile both white and brown meat back into the cleaned out carapace for serving 'dressed'. This looks impressive and makes a delicious starter or lunch dish with a salad and warmed bread. Twist off the claws and legs and set aside. You're left with two shells, the larger head shell and the smaller body shell that the legs were attached to. Holding the head shell towards you, push the body shell away from you with your thumbs until it's completely detached.

On each side of the body shell are two rows of feathery gills known as 'dead men's fingers'. Pull these away and discard them. The two inedible parts in the head shell include the transparent papery-looking stomach sac and the hard bony bits behind the eyes. Theses both pull away easily. The inedible parts have now all been discarded.

Using a large sharp knife, cut the body shell firmly in half. Scoop out as much of the white meat as you can using the tip of a skewer to reach into all the little cavities. Once the meat has been removed from both halves, you should be able to see right through all the little cavities and tunnels in the shell.

Scoop the brown meat from the head shell and put in a separate bowl. You'll find that the texture of the brown meat will vary from being quite firm around the edges to soft in the centre. Don't discard any of these as all parts are edible and delicious.

Using a hammer, crack open the claws and legs so that you can get to the white meat inside. Scoop it into the bowl of white meat.

To serve the crab in its shell, tap along the clearly defined curvy white line on the underside of the head shell. The inner edges should break away leaving you with a container with clean edges that can be used to hold the meat. Wash it well and dry it. Beat a little mayonnaise and pepper into the brown meat until it's broken up and smooth. Spoon across the centre of the shell. Flake the white meat with a fork and pack down each side of the brown meat. Finely chop some parsley, a little hard-boiled egg white and hard-boiled egg yolk, chopped separately. Arrange in lines across the brown meat to garnish.

Cleaning squid

Squid can usually be bought as tubes (cleaned bodies), or rings (sliced tubes). Sometimes the heads are tucked into the cleaned bodies when you buy them. Use the squid bodies whole (this is perfect if they're about 10–12 cm (4–4¾ in) long and you intend to stuff them,) or slice them into rings, which is great for frying. Alternatively cut along one side of the squid body so you can open it out into a flat piece. Here's how to prepare a whole squid.

Pull the head and tentacles away from the body. Squeeze out the contents of the body. This includes a jelly-like substance and a transparent quill-like cartilage.

Insert a thumb under the wings and pull away. (On smaller squid these can simply be pulled away with your fingers). Reserve these as they can also be cooked.

Run the squid under cold water, then rub off the mottled skin with your thumbs. Cut between the eyes and the tentacles so the tentacles remain in one piece. Discard the head. Pat dry.

To open the squid out flat, insert the knife into the inside of the tube and cut along the line left by the quill

Scoring shallow cuts 2 cm (¾ in) apart, helps to keep the squid tender and cook quickly. (Make sure you don't cut right through the flesh).

How to tell if fish is cooked through

Fish cooks quickly because it doesn't have as much muscle and connective tissue as meat. What it does have breaks down quickly, even on more active deep-water fish such as tuna. There are no complications of having to deal with tough or tender cuts with fish cooking. When a fish is cooked through to the centre it's done – it's as simple as that! The time taken will depend on the cooking method and the thickness of the fish. A piece of fillet cooked in hot liquid will be cooked through in a few minutes, whereas a whole grilled or baked fish will take longer. Basically, fish is cooked when the flesh has turned from a translucent colour to an opaque one, whether it's pure white, or varying tones of pink in the case of salmon or trout. On a whole fish the flesh should readily come away from the bone. All the recipes give guidelines as to how long the fish will take but you'll need to do your own test to be certain. The easiest method is to push the tip of a knife into the thickest area of the fish. The flesh should part easily and should be of an even colour right through.

Using a thermometer

This is useful if you're cooking large pieces of fish or whole fish that might be wrapped in bacon or other ingredients. It's the same type of thermometer that you'd use to test whether meat is cooked to the right temperature and consists of a metal probe and temperature gauge. Push the probe into the thickest area of the fish and leave for a few seconds. Fish is cooked through when the internal temperature reaches about 55°C (131°F). If you don't have a thermometer you can also gauge whether or not it is cooked by pushing a metal skewer into the fish. Leave for 10 seconds and remove. The tip should feel hot to the touch, but not burning hot!

The only exception to the 'cooked through' rule is the cooking of fish such as tuna that you might want to serve rare.

Baking and Roasting

Using the oven to cook fish produces some of the most versatile results, from stuffed and wrapped fish dishes to pies, bakes and roasts. Fillets or whole fish can be cooked fast with dry heat, or slowly and gently by combining them with other ingredients that help to stop the fish from drying out. Use the oven when you've a large whole fish or fillets that you want to cook as one impressive 'joint'. Such dishes are great for entertaining because you'll have done all the preparation in advance so all that's left to do is to pop the dish in the oven, then serve it once its ready.

The terms 'baking' and 'roasting' with regard to fish are fairly interchangeable. Baked dishes are usually cooked more gently than roasted dishes and the fish is combined with other ingredients such as a sauce, vegetables, cheese, gratin or crumble topping. The dish is usually a deep-sided baking dish rather than a roasting pan so it can be taken direct to the table for serving. Baked fish dishes make perfect wintry comfort food.

Roasted fish is generally cooked in a hot oven so the fish cooks quickly on the outside, keeping the centre moist and juicy. Because the heat is intense the fish needs to be wrapped in or topped with ingredients that will stop it drying out. Cured ham such as Prosciutto or Serrano, or thin-cut bacon is ideal, crisping as it cooks and imparting its flavour to the fish it envelops. A good smothering of butter or olive oil is also effective. Flavour-packed stuffings add extra taste to a chunky piece of fish, or you can tuck in additional ingredients such as garlic, herbs and spices. Alternatively, resting the fish as it cooks over a bed of sliced onions, shallot or fennel, for example, adds flavour, particularly if you will be using the pan juices to make an accompanying sauce. You can even make deep cuts into a large piece of fish, or whole fish, and stuff herbs and garlic into the slits just as you might do for meat.

After roasting, the pan juices can be cooked on the hob with reduced fish stock, wine and cream to make a sauce.

To make a sauce with roasting juices

Transfer the roasted fish to a warmed serving plate. Heat the roasting tin on the hob, adding some well flavoured fish stock, white wine or a mixture of the two. Let the mixture bubble up until the liquid has reduced to intensify the flavour. Swirl in a little cream or crème fraîche, some finely chopped fresh parsley, tarragon, dill, chervil or fennel to make a simple, but delicious, sauce. Taste to test the seasoning, and add salt and pepper, if needed, before you serve.

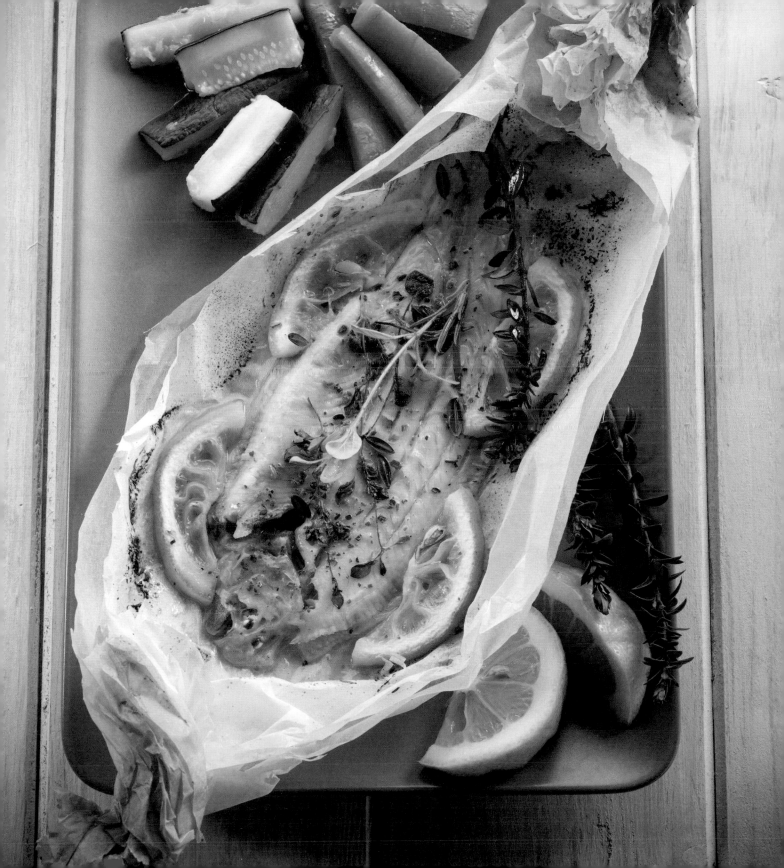

Baking fish in paper

This classic style of baking is called 'en papillote', meaning baking 'in a parcel'. The idea is to keep the fish moist by trapping steam within the paper bag and allowing the flavours of the ingredients that you've added to it to mingle. Kitchen foil parcels work well too, but paper ones look more attractive as they puff up and colour during baking. You can remove the fish from the bags and transfer to serving plates or transfer the bags to serving plates so everyone can open their own.

For each serving cut out a 28cm (11in) circle of greaseproof paper (baking parchment) and grease the centre of each with a little butter. Place a piece of fish – a chunky fillet of white fish or salmon is ideal – on one half of the circle, dot with extra butter and add aromatic ingredients such as chopped shallots, fresh herbs, capers, lemon rind, crushed green peppercorns and a little seasoning. Alternatively, try an Asian-inspired version with spring onions (scallions), coriander (cilantro), finely chopped fresh ginger, lemongrass and a drizzle of soy sauce. Fold the free half of the paper circle over the fish so that the edges meet. Starting at one side of the semi-circle, fold the paper edges over once or twice to secure them firmly together and work around the parcel, folding as you go until completely sealed. Transfer to a baking sheet and brush the paper with more butter. Bake at 200°C/400°F/Gas Mark 6 for about 15 minutes or until the fish is cooked. To test, make a slit in the top of one parcel and push a knife down into the thickest area of the fish to see if it's cooked through.

If you use foil for baking fish portions, extend the cooking time slightly as the heat won't penetrate foil as quickly as paper. Cut squares, rather than circles and simply fold over and crimp around the edges. This is a useful technique for healthy midweek eating when you might want to add ingredients like sliced tomatoes and garlic, chopped parsley or basil, pitted olives or capers and a drizzle of olive oil.

Baking and roasting tips

• Any whole fish can be baked successfully, provided it fits neatly into the pan or baking dish. Position diagonally or cut off the head if necessary so the fish fits neatly in the container.

• If cooking a whole fish, butter or grease the dish or pan well before positioning the fish, particularly where the head, fins and tail rest, otherwise they'll bake onto the dish and will be difficult to remove for serving.

• Never roast fish without additional ingredients to keep it moist. Brushing the raw fish with oil or melted butter, seasoning with salt and pepper and adding garlic or herbs will keep the fish moist and make a simple dish that needs no other embellishment.

• Baking and roasting are great cooking methods for oily fish as their natural oils keep them beautifully moist. Simply tuck a few herbs and lemon slices into the cavity of a whole fish or underneath the fish portions for an easy roast. A flavoured mayonnaise or tomato sauce makes a lovely accompaniment.

• Scoring whole fish or fillets will accelerate cooking times and allow flavours to be absorbed.

• A moderate oven set to 180°C/350°F/Gas Mark 4 is ideal for baking fish with additional ingredients such as potatoes and other vegetables. At this temperature thin fish fillets, for example flat fish, will take about 8 minutes, chunky fish fillets of about 3cm (1¼ in) thickness will take about 12–15 minutes and whole, single portion sized fish, about 20 minutes. Because fish cooks quickly you'll need to pre-cook any vegetables to a stage where they're almost cooked through before adding the fish.

• Using the oven means you don't have to oversee cooking continuously so it's quite a relaxed form of cooking.

• As the oven is in use, think about vegetables that can be oven cooked at the same time. Jacket or roasted potatoes and any other roasted root vegetables make good accompaniments. Bake these first to a point where they're pale golden and softened, then put them on the lower shelf while you cook the fish above.

fish pie

Fish pies take a little more time to prepare than most fish dishes but you'll love the results – a creamy sauce with cheesy mash and a crispy crust, pure comfort food indulgence and a dish that you can cook time and time again. It can also be made ahead, up to a day in advance and chilled so you only need to pop it in the oven when you're ready and serve as it is, or with seasonal vegetables.

Serves 6

1 kg (2¼ lb) white fish fillets, such as pollack, whiting, haddock or cod

300 ml (½ pint) milk

6 eggs, soft boiled and shelled

1 kg (2¼ lb) floury potatoes, peeled and chopped into large chunks

100 g (3½ oz) Cheddar cheese, or other strong hard cheese, grated

100 g (3½ oz) unsalted butter

1 onion, chopped

2 tablespoons plain (all purpose) flour

150 ml (¼ pint) double (heavy) cream

6 tablespoons finely chopped fresh herbs, such as parsley, dill or tarragon

25 g (1 oz) breadcrumbs

salt and freshly ground black pepper

To poach the fish, place the fillets in a single layer in a large frying pan and add the milk. Bring to a gentle simmer and partially cover with a lid. Cook very gently for about 5 minutes, or until the fish separates easily into flakes. Set aside until cool enough to handle. Remove the fish and put on a plate. Reserve the milk for the sauce. Pull the fish into large pieces, discarding the skin and any bones. Place in a shallow ovenproof dish and arrange the eggs over the top. Preheat the oven to 190°C/375°F/Gas Mark 5.

In a large pan of lightly salted boiling water, cook the potatoes for 15–20 minutes, or until tender. Drain and return to the pan. Mash well, adding half the cheese, half the butter and a dash of the reserved milk.

Meanwhile, to make the sauce, melt 25 g (1 oz) of the butter in a clean pan over a medium heat, add the onion and gently fry for 5 minutes to soften. Add the flour, beating it with a wooden spoon until no lumps of flour remain. Remove from the heat and gradually blend in the rest of the reserved milk, beating with a wooden spoon or whisk until smooth. Stir in the cream, return to the heat and cook gently, stirring until the sauce has thickened. Stir in the herbs, and season with salt and pepper to taste. Pour about three-quarters over the fish.

Spoon the mash on top of the filling, adding plenty of peaks and dips with a fork. Spoon over the remaining sauce and sprinkle the remaining cheese on top. Melt the remaining butter in a small pan. Stir in the breadcrumbs and sprinkle over the top of the pie. Bake for about 45 minutes, or until deep golden.

cockle and bacon gratin

੭੭

This recipe is easy to make as well as economical – an ideal dish for midweek eating. Cockles and bacon always make a tasty combination, or you could substitute cooked prawns for the cockles, or leave out the bacon altogether. Make sure that the cockles you use have not been preserved in vinegar as this will affect the consistency of the sauce.

Serves 4

butter, for greasing

750 g (1 lb 10 oz) small waxy potatoes, scrubbed and thinly sliced

100 g (3½ oz) streaky (fatty) bacon, finely diced

200 g (7 oz) cooked and shelled cockles

250 ml (8 fl oz) double (heavy) cream

250 ml (8 fl oz) full fat (whole) milk

1 tablespoon finely chopped fresh thyme

2 garlic cloves, peeled and crushed

50g (2oz) Gruyère cheese, finely grated

salt and freshly ground black pepper

1 onion, thinly sliced

Preheat the oven to 180°C/350°F/Gas Mark 4. Generously butter a shallow ovenproof dish.

Put the sliced potatoes in a large pan of lightly salted boiling water. Return to the boil, then boil for 5 minutes or until the slices feel soft when pierced with a knife. Drain in a colander.

Fry the bacon in a dry frying pan for 6–8 minutes, stirring frequently until the pieces are crisp and deep golden.

Drain and rinse the cockles if sold in brine. Pat dry on kitchen paper.

In a small bowl, beat together the cream, milk, thyme, garlic and half the cheese. Season with plenty of black pepper.

Arrange half the potatoes in the ovenproof dish and scatter with the onion slices, bacon and cockles. Arrange the remaining potatoes on top and pour over the cream mixture. Scatter with the remaining cheese and bake for about 1 hour or until the potatoes are tender and the crust is golden

tapas prawns

A look at the ingredients list here is a sure sign that the results will be good! This dish is easy to put together and makes a great starter for a casual supper or a delicious snack – just make sure you leave enough time for marinating the prawns. Small, individual ovenproof dishes are perfect for tapas, or use one larger one, if you like.

Serves 4

450 g (1 lb) raw shell-on prawns

2 garlic cloves, peeled and sliced

1 medium strength red chilli, de-seeded
   and finely chopped

200 ml (7 fl oz) extra virgin olive oil

salt

warmed rustic bread, to serve

Arrange the prawns in a large shallow ovenproof dish. Sprinkle with the garlic and chilli, then spoon over the oil. Cover loosely and leave to marinate for 1–2 hours before cooking. Preheat the oven to 180°C/350°F/Gas Mark 4.

Place the dish on a baking tray, put in the oven and cook for about 20 minutes or until the prawns have turned completely pink. Leave to cool slightly and serve with chunks of warm bread for mopping up the flavoured oil.

one-pot fish roast

This recipe combines fish and vegetables in one pan so you'll have no additional preparation to do other than mixing a few salad leaves as an accompaniment, if you like. Sea bass roasts beautifully, but you can substitute any other firm-textured white fish fillets.

Serves 4

4 small onions, peeled

500 g (1¼ lb) small, whole beetroots

500 g (1¼ lb) small new potatoes, scrubbed

1 tablespoon finely chopped fresh rosemary, plus
    extra to garnish

¼ teaspoon celery salt

1 garlic bulb

75 ml (5 tablespoons) olive oil

4 sea bass fillets, skin on, each weighing 150–175 g
    (5–6 oz)

salt and freshly ground black pepper

100 g (3 ½ oz) crème fraîche

45 ml (3 tablespoons) hot horseradish sauce

Preheat the oven to 220°C/425°F/Gas Mark 7. Cut the onions into chunky wedges. Place them in a heatproof bowl, cover with boiling water and leave to stand for 2 minutes. Drain, rinse under cold running water and peel away the softened skins. Scrub the beetroots, and cut into even wedges. Arrange in a large roasting pan with the onions and potatoes. Sprinkle the rosemary and the celery salt over the vegetables. Separate the garlic cloves and add to the pan. Drizzle with 60ml (4 tablespoons) of the olive oil and roast for about 50 minutes, turning the vegetables once or twice during cooking until they're soft and lightly roasted.

Score the fish fillets, and season with salt and pepper. Add to the roasting pan, nestling them among the vegetables. Drizzle the fish with the remaining oil and scatter with more rosemary sprigs. Return to the oven for 15 minutes or until the fish is cooked through.

In a small bowl, beat together the crème fraîche and the horseradish and tip into a small serving dish. Transfer the fish and vegetables to serving plates and serve with the sauce.

salt-crusted fish with garlic or saffron mayonnaise

੭Ꮼ

Don't be put off by the amount of salt used in this recipe – it's used to seal the fish, trapping flavour and moisture inside and adding subtle seasoning while it bakes. Afterwards, the salt crust is lifted off and the fish is served simply as it is. To accompany this dish all you need are buttered new potatoes and a tomato or leafy salad.

Serves 4

1 whole, firm-textured white fish, such as sea bream, snapper or sea bass, gutted, scaled, about 1.25 kg (2½ lb)

freshly ground black pepper

2 limes, scrubbed and sliced

small handful of fresh thyme and fresh parsley sprigs

1.5kg (3lb 5oz) coarse sea salt

Garlic or Saffron Mayonnaise, to serve, see Basic Recipes

Preheat the oven to 200°C/400°F/Gas Mark 6. Line a roasting pan with a large sheet of heavy-duty kitchen foil, leaving a little foil overhanging the ends of the pan. Scatter a thin layer of salt into the base.

Rinse the fish (but do not pat dry) and arrange on the salt, fitting diagonally in the tin, if necessary. Season the fish inside and out with black pepper and tuck the lime slices and herbs into the cavity.

Pull up the foil around the fish so that there is about 2 cm (¾ in) of space between fish and foil. Tip in the remaining salt until the fish is completely covered. Drizzle the salt with 100 ml (3½ fl oz) cold water (use your hands to do this). Bake for 25 minutes.

Remove from the oven. To check that the fish is cooked, lift away enough of the salt to reveal some of the fish. Test the fish is cooked through. (If necessary, cover with foil and return to the oven for a few more minutes.) When you are satisfied that the fish is cooked, leave to stand for 10 minutes then lift away all the salt crust, which should come away in large pieces.

Peel away the fish skin. Carefully lift the top fillet from the upper side of the bone and put on serving plates, then remove the backbone and serve the lower fillet. Accompany with the mayonnaise.

Serrano-wrapped roasted monkfish

For a dish that's a little bit special, try this combination of firm-textured white fish with salty cured meat – it's fabulous! Serve with buttered new potatoes or creamy mash and a seasonal vegetable. A tray of well-flavoured tomatoes, halved and roasted with a drizzle of olive oil under the fish is also really good.

Serves 6

2 x 750 g (1 lb 10 oz) monkfish fillets

3 garlic cloves, peeled and crushed

2 tablespoons finely chopped fresh parsley

1 tablespoon finely chopped fresh thyme

finely grated rind of 1 lemon

60 ml (4 tablespoons) olive oil

6 slices Serrano ham

300 ml (½ pint) fish stock

100 ml (3½ fl oz) double (heavy) cream

salt and freshly ground black pepper

Preheat the oven to 200°C/400°F/Gas Mark 6. Remove any dark areas of membrane from the monkfish fillets. Brush the base of a roasting pan with a little oil.

In a small bowl, mix together the garlic, parsley, thyme, lemon rind and a little seasoning. Rub along the surface of one monkfish fillet. Drizzle with 1 tablespoon of the oil. Arrange the second fillet on top so that a thick end is against a thin end to keep the shape uniform.

Wrap the slices of Serrano ham around the fish, tucking the ends underneath and keeping the slices evenly spaced down the length of the fillets. Tie lengths of fine string around the ham-wrapped fish to hold the ingredients together. Transfer to the roasting pan and drizzle with the remaining oil. Roast for 25 minutes or until the fish is cooked through.

Lift the fish out onto a serving platter, remove the string, and keep warm. Add the fish stock to the roasting pan and cook on the hob over a high heat until the liquid is reduced by about half. Pour in the cream and heat through, stirring frequently. Season to taste and pour into a serving jug. Thickly slice the fish and serve with the sauce.

paper-wrapped halibut with tomatoes and Parmesan

૭૦૩

Cooking fish in a paper parcel is a perfect method for very fresh, chunky pieces of fillet – a light and healthy dish that is packed with flavour. The fish parcel contains simple ingredients that enhance, rather than overpower, the fish.

Serves 2

40 g (1½ oz) butter

1 shallot, thinly sliced

2 x 175–200 g (6–7 oz) chunky fillets, such as
    halibut or blue eye cod steaks

1 garlic clove, peeled and thinly sliced

50 g (2 oz) semi-dried tomatoes in oil, drained
    and chopped

2 tablespoons chopped fresh parsley

40 g (1½ oz) freshly grated Parmesan cheese

salt and freshly ground black pepper

Preheat the oven to 200°C/400°F/Gas Mark 6. Cut two 28 cm (11 in) circles of baking parchment. Melt the butter in a small pan. Generously brush the paper circles to within 5 cm (2 in) of the edges with a little of the butter.

Tip the shallot into a small pan of boiling water and cook for 1 minute, drain.

Season the halibut fillets and arrange on one half of each piece of paper. Scatter the shallot, garlic, tomatoes and parsley on top. Drizzle with a little more butter, reserving a little for brushing. Season with salt and pepper and sprinkle with the Parmesan.

Fold the paper over the filling and secure the edges together. Slide onto a baking sheet and brush with the paper the remaining butter. Bake for 20 minutes. Transfer to serving plates and serve with buttered potatoes and herb or rocket (arugula) salad.

seafood crumble

Making a fish crumble is much the same as a pastry-lidded fish pie, but easier. The crumble ingredients are simply scattered over the filling for a simple 'one pot' supper dish. No other accompaniments required!

Serves 4

500 g (1¼ lb) firm white fish fillets e.g. tilapia, mahi mahi, skinned

200 g (7 oz) cooked and peeled prawns

50 g (2 oz) butter

1 onion, chopped

250 g (9 oz) chestnut mushrooms, sliced

2 tablespoons plain (all-purpose) flour

300 ml (½ pint) milk

150 ml (¼ pint) single (light) cream

salt and freshly ground black pepper

FOR THE CRUMBLE

150 g (5 oz) plain (all-purpose) flour

100 g (3 ½ oz) lightly salted butter, diced

50 g (2 oz) freshly grated Parmesan cheese

Preheat the oven to 180°C/350°F/Gas Mark 4. Cut each fish fillet into large pieces and arrange in a shallow ovenproof dish with the prawns, or use individual dishes.

To make the sauce, melt the butter in a small pan over a medium heat, add the onion and fry gently for 5 minutes. Add the mushrooms and fry, stirring for another 2 minutes. Sprinkle in the flour and mix with a wooden spoon for 1 minute. Remove from the heat and gradually blend in the milk, beating well until smooth and no lumps of flour remain. Stir in the cream and a little seasoning and return to the heat. Cook gently, stirring until the sauce has thickened. Tip out over the fish and prawns.

For the crumble, put the flour in a food processor and add the butter. Blend until the mixture resembles fine breadcrumbs. (Alternatively put the flour in a bowl, add the butter and rub in with the fingertips.) Add the Parmesan and blend a little more until the mixture starts to make large crumbly pieces. Tip out onto the filling and spread to the edges.

Bake for about 40 minutes or until the crumble is pale golden and the sauce is bubbling up around the edges.

trout with bacon and lemongrass

Bacon and fish make delicious partners, particularly with trout, which can have a slightly earthy taste. Citrus flavours such as lemongrass give extra zing.

Serves 2

25 g (1 oz) butter, plus extra to grease

2 medium trout, heads removed, if liked

1 stalk lemongrass

salt and freshly ground black pepper

45 ml (3 tablespoons) wok, stir fry or groundnut oil

75 g (3 oz) smoked streaky (fatty) bacon,
    finely diced

Preheat the oven to 180°C/350°F/Gas Mark 4. Grease a shallow ovenproof dish or roasting pan with butter.

Score the trout several times down each side, and place in the dish.

Pull away any tough outer layers from the lemongrass and discard the ends. Cut in half lengthways then chop as finely as possible. Place half in the fish cavities along with a little salt and pepper.

Heat the oil in a small frying pan and fry the bacon until crisp, about 5 minutes. Add the remaining lemongrass to the pan and cook for 30 seconds. Spoon the mixture over the fish and drizzle with the juices from the pan. Bake for 20 minutes or until the fish is cooked through.

roasted mackerel with Asian butter

Mackerel is great for baking whole, particularly if you choose smallish fish so each is a perfect single portion size. A larger mackerel weighing about 450 g or 1 lb will easily serve two people. The tangy, citrus-flavoured butter helps balance the richness of the fish.

Serves 2

40 g (1½ oz) unsalted butter, softened, plus
    extra to grease

2 small whole mackerel, boned if liked, and
    heads removed

10 g (¼ oz) piece fresh root ginger,
    grated (shredded)

1 garlic clove, crushed

½ teaspoon five-spice powder

finely grated rind of 1 lime, plus 1 teaspoon juice

3 tablespoons finely chopped fresh coriander
    (cilantro)

salt and freshly ground black pepper

lime wedges, to serve

Preheat the oven to 200°C/400°F/Gas Mark 6. Grease a shallow ovenproof dish or roasting pan with butter.

To make the Asian butter, mix the butter in a bowl with the ginger, garlic, five spice powder, lime zest and juice, 2 tablespoons of the coriander and a little salt and pepper. Spread a little down each side of the mackerel.

Place the fish in the dish and dot a little more butter along the upper fillets. Roast for 20 minutes or until the fish is cooked through. Serve sprinkled with the remaining coriander and topped with the remaining butter.

roasted fish with chorizo stuffing

The stuffing for this dish is well flavoured and fiery, perfect for jazzing up everyday white fish such as whiting, ling, pollack or coley.

Serves 4

100 g (3 ½ oz) chorizo

50 g (2 oz) breadcrumbs

30 ml (2 tablespoons) sun-dried tomato paste

45 ml (3 tablespoons) olive oil

1 tablespoon finely chopped fresh thyme, plus extra sprigs to garnish

2 x 400 g (14 oz) white fish fillets, skin and bones removed

300 g (11 oz) cherry tomatoes, halved

salt and freshly ground black pepper

Preheat the oven to 200°C/400°F/Gas Mark 6. Chop the chorizo into small pieces and blend in a food processor until finely chopped. Add the breadcrumbs, tomato paste, 15 ml (1 tablespoon) of the oil, the chopped thyme and a little salt and pepper, and blend lightly to combine.

Lightly oil a shallow baking dish. Spread the stuffing along one fillet. Arrange the other fillet on top so that a thick end is against a thin end to keep the shape uniform. Tie string around the fish at 5 cm (2 in) intervals to hold the fillets together as it cooks. Transfer to the dish.

Scatter the tomatoes around the fish and drizzle both fish and tomatoes with the remaining oil. Season lightly with salt and pepper and scatter with thyme sprigs. Cook for 25 minutes or until the fish is cooked through..

baked bream with fennel and red onions

This dish looks and tastes so special and couldn't be easier to put together. Pile the vegetables onto serving plates, place the fish on top and sprinkle with extra parsley for a professional-looking treat of a supper.

Serves 2

1 head fennel

1 red onion, thinly sliced

60 ml (4 tablespoons) olive oil

salt and freshly ground black pepper

2 x 250 g (9 oz) fillets of bream, snapper or mullet

8 pitted black olives

3 anchovy fillets from a can, drained and chopped

15 ml (1 tablespoon) lemon juice

2 tablespoons finely chopped fresh parsley

Preheat the oven to 180°C/350°F/Gas Mark 4. Thinly slice the fennel, discarding the core and scatter into a shallow ovenproof dish with the onion. Drizzle with 15 ml (1 tablespoon) of the oil and add a little salt and pepper. Bake for 15 minutes to lightly soften the vegetables.

Score the fish fillet, and arrange each over the vegetables. Add the olives, cover with foil and bake for 15 minutes.

Meanwhile mix the remaining oil with the anchovy fillets, lemon juice, parsley and a little ground black pepper. Remove the foil and spoon the dressing over the fish and vegetables. Return to the oven for another 5 minutes before serving.

gurnard with hot Greek salad

This fish is a great favourite in soups and stews in which the fish bones flavour the stock, and the filleted flesh is added late in the cooking process. In this recipe only the fillets are used, but ask the fishmonger to give you the bones for making stock, if you like. Large herring fillets or whole sardines (photographed here) are also delicious when used in this recipe and will take a similar time to cook.

Serves 4

6 tomatoes

1 green (bell) pepper, de-seeded and cut
    into chunks

½ red onion, thinly sliced

90 ml (6 tablespoons) extra virgin olive oil

2 garlic cloves, peeled and crushed

salt and freshly ground black pepper

200 g (7 oz) feta cheese, diced

rosemary sprigs

4 red or grey gurnard fillets

4 pitta breads or flatbreads, warmed on the lower
    shelf of the oven for 5 minutes, to serve

Preheat the oven to 200°C/400°F/Gas Mark 6. Roughly chop the tomatoes and place in a small, shallow ovenproof dish. Add the green pepper and red onion.

Mix 60 ml (4 tablespoons) of the olive oil with the garlic and drizzle over the salad. Season with salt and pepper. Scatter the diced feta cheese on top. Bake for 5 minutes.

Line a small baking sheet with kitchen foil. Brush with a little oil and scatter with rosemary sprigs. (Both the salad dish and baking sheet should fit on the same shelf in the oven. The baking sheet can rest under the dish but keep the rosemary to one side of the baking sheet so the salad isn't resting on it.)

Score the fish down each side, and season with salt and pepper. Rest the fish over the rosemary sprigs and drizzle with the remaining oil. Place both salad and fish in the oven and cook for about 15 minutes until the fish is cooked through, and the salad is hot. Serve with the pitta bread

Grilling
and barbecuing

As soon as the weather heats up, out comes the barbecue and what we eat and the way we eat it becomes so much more relaxed and leisurely. The senses and smells associated with barbecuing might gear us up into holiday mood or let us re-live culinary experiences already enjoyed. It's a fun and easy way to cook, though most of us are still wary of barbecuing fish when it seems so much easier to whack a few burgers, sausages or steaks over the coals. The truth is that barbecuing fish is easier than meat. It cooks through to the centre quickly and there's less chance of serving food that's cindered on the outside and dubiously raw in the centre. The flavour is also unbeatable as fish readily absorbs the smokiness and the skin crisps perfectly.

The technique for grilling fish is basically the same. Both methods cook fast and with an intense, dry heat. Oily fish, by nature, grills and barbecues well, staying moist and juicy. Salmon, trout, mackerel and sardines are great 'oily' favourites, though white fish and shellfish can also work brilliantly. The secret is to avoid overcooking. Keep a close eye on the fish, piercing the thickest area of flesh frequently to see if it's nearly there. The intense heat will quickly spoil overcooked fish, rendering it dry and disappointing

Bastes, marinades, rubs and butters

Grilling and barbecuing are great methods for the cook who's willing to experiment. Here's your chance to steep fish in simple marinades, rub it with herb or spice blends, or make delicious flavoured butters that melt over cooked fish once plated up. Ingredients like garlic, citrus rind, horseradish sauce, spring onions (scallions), capers, chilli, parsley, chives, tarragon, dill, fennel, lovage, coriander (cilantro), basil, cumin and cardamom are all delicious with fish so devise your own recipes depending on what you have to hand. Keep it simple and you can't go wrong.

dill, mustard and caper marinade

Perfect for salmon and white fish fillets.

3 tablespoons finely chopped fresh dill

15 ml (1 tablespoon) grainy mustard

1 tablespoon rinsed, drained and chopped capers

1 tablespoon caster (superfine) sugar

finely grated rind of 1 lemon and 15ml (1 tablespoon) juice

45 ml (3 tablespoons) olive oil

salt and freshly ground black pepper

Mix the dill in a bowl with the mustard, capers, sugar, lemon rind and juice, oil and a little seasoning. Place the fish in a non-metallic dish and spoon the marinade over. Turn the fish to coat and leave to marinate for 15–30 minutes before cooking.

blue cheese and chive buttter

A delicious topping for small white fish fillets or flat fish.

120 g (4 oz) unsalted butter, softened

75 g (3 oz) creamy Stilton, crumbled

freshly ground black pepper

45 ml (3 tablespoons) finely chopped fresh chives.

Put the butter, Stilton and plenty of black pepper in a food processor or blender and blend until mixed. Lightly stir in the herbs. Transfer to a small serving dish ready to spoon over the cooked fish.

chilli, garlic and soy baste

Try with firm textured white fish, salmon, prawns, squid or scallops.

1 small red chilli, de-seeded and finely chopped

1 garlic clove, peeled and crushed

½ teaspoon ground coriander

15 ml (1 tablespoon) clear honey

15 ml (1 tablespoon) wine vinegar

30 ml (2 tablespoons) soy sauce

Mix all the ingredients together in a small bowl. Brush over the fish during cooking.

citrus spice rub

For oily fish such as mackerel, salmon, sardines, herrings and sprats.

rind of 1 orange

5 ml (1 teaspoon) cumin seeds, crushed

5 ml (1 teaspoon) coriander seeds, crushed

seeds of 10 cardamom pods, crushed

½ teaspoon freshly ground black pepper

pinch of salt

Mix all the ingredients together in a small bowl. Rub over the fish just before cooking.

Using a grill

Sometimes, when you've bought an expensive piece of fish, or whole fish and you want to enjoy it completely unadulterated, grilling (broiling) it is the easiest and most sympathetic way to cook it. Whole flat fish such as Dover sole, lemon sole, plaice, dabs, flounder and witch all respond well to this form of cooking. Simply serve topped with a pat of butter, squeeze of lemon and light seasoning, or a flavoured oil.

To cook, preheat the grill and line a grill rack or baking sheet with foil. Brush the foil with melted butter or oil. (This will prevent the fish head, fins and tail from baking onto the foil as it cooks). Place the fish or fishes on the foil and season lightly. (If grilling skin on fish portions or flat fish, position with the dark skin side face down, unless you're grilling skinned Dover sole, in which case grill with the skinned side face down). Brush with a little melted butter or olive oil and grill, keeping a fairly close eye on the fish. As a guide, allow about 4 minutes each side for a chunky fillet or cutlet of about 3–4cm (1¼ –1 ¾ in) thickness. For a medium sized flat fish, allow 5-6 minutes each side, turning once. Brush the fish with more butter or oil and seasoning once you're turned it

Preparing the barbecue

It is essential to prepare the barbecue properly before you start to cook. Cremated fish is a sure sign that the barbecue was too hot when you started cooking. Light the barbecue 20–30 minutes beforehand so that the coals are gently glowing rather than throwing up flames.

It's best to use lumpwood charcoal rather than the fuel-injected charcoal briquettes, which create a very intense heat. Lumpwood charcoal is natural charcoal whereas the briquettes are injected with fuel to make them burn hotter. Use any size of barbecue from small portable ones to those that have a fixed place in the garden. Many keen barbecue cooks prefer gas barbecues as they're cleaner and the supply of gas from a canister will last longer than several sacks of charcoal. The cooking temperature can be raised or lowered as you would when cooking using a conventional cooker. Gas barbecues, however, won't permeate the fish with lovely smoky flavours. They're also more expensive.

You don't need any specific utensils for barbecuing fish, though a 'fish rack', see below, is great for cooking whole fish. A pair of long-handled tongs is useful for turning pieces of fish. Long-handled forks are not used as much for fish barbecuing as they are for meat as fish will easily break up if repeatedly pierced. You'll also find a sturdy scourer useful for cleaning up the barbecue of fish skins and pieces of fish that cling obstinately to the rack.

Once you're happy that the fire has died down position the barbecue rack so that it can heat up before you add the fish. The intensity of the heat can be adjusted by lifting the cooking rack higher or moving the food to the sides of the barbecue where the heat might not be as intense as it is at the centre. If fat drips down onto the coals and causes a flare up use a squirt of water to douse the flames. It's worth getting a spray bottle and filing it with water just in case.

Using barbecue racks

As it cooks, fish, whether whole or filleted, becomes more fragile and prone to falling apart no matter how much care you take when manoeuvring it around. Hinged barbecue grill racks, available in various sizes for cooking small or large whole fish, make easy work of turning fish while cooking. Once you've seasoned and oiled your fish, place it in the rack and rest it over the barbecue grill, checking the fish and turning the rack as required.

Using a ridged pan (char-grill)

Ridged grill pans (also sometimes called griddles) are used on the hob but create the effect of barbecuing as the fish is seared with lightly charred lines. They take longer to heat than a regular frying pan and must be very hot before cooking or your fish fillets, steaks or whole fish are very likely to stick to the pan. Brush the fish with oil before adding to the pan and let it cook completely on the underside, undisturbed, before turning it. If you keep moving the fish around you won't end up with the well-defined lines associated with this technique and it'll look messy and unprofessional. To see whether the fish is cooked on the underside, carefully lift one end before turning the whole lot. If it needs longer, put the fish back down in exactly the same position.

Grilling and barbecuing tips

• Line the grill (broiler) rack with foil to make cleaning up easier after cooking fish.

• Make sure the barbecue, grill or ridged pan is preheated before adding the fish so it sears quickly, retaining all its flavour and juices. If using a barbecue the flames should have died down and the coals be gently glowing before adding any fish.

• Once chunky pieces of fish have crisped on the outside but are still raw in the centre, you can turn the heat down or transfer the fish to a less hot area of the barbecue.

• Brush the surface of the fish with oil before cooking, rather than the grill rack or barbecue rack. This will help prevent it sticking, or stop flare ups from occurring if barbecuing. Pay particular attention to the heads, fins and tails as these are the most likely to stick.

• Scoring fillets or whole fish along each side will accelerate cooking and help any flavourings or seasoning permeate the fish.

• Grilling and barbecuing cooking times vary according to the type of fish, thickness and heat intensity which is not regulated as it is for oven cooking. As a general guide a thin fillet such as plaice or red mullet will take 2 minutes each side. (If it is too fragile to turn cook one side only for 3–4 minutes.) A plump fillet like salmon or cod will take 3–4 minutes each side, and a whole portion sized fish,about 275–300 g (10–12 oz), about 6 minutes each side.

• Shellfish like scallops and prawns can be cooked on wooden or metal skewers so they're easier to turn. Leave a space between each item to let the heat circulate.

• If barbecuing small fish such as sardines or sprats, thread a long skewer just below the heads of the fish and then another just above the tails to create a ladder arrangement. This will make the whole lot easier to turn in one go.

• If using wooden skewers, soak them in hot water for 30 minutes prior to threading so the wood doesn't burn as quickly.

• Scatter plenty of hardy herbs such as thyme, rosemary and bay leaves onto the coals from time to time. These enhance the flavour of the fish and smell delicious!

• Fish grills and barbecues surprisingly quickly. Never leave the fish unattended.

• Marinades and rubs are great for adding flavour prior to cooking. You can also baste fish with herb- or spice-infused oils as it cooks. As an alternative to a pastry brush tie a large bunch of thyme with string, leave it in a dish of olive oil for a couple of hours, or longer, before you start cooking and use it as a basting tool so that you're adding extra flavour when basting the fish with the oil.

grilled sardines with herb salt

To enjoy sardines at their best it's vital that you cook really fresh ones since they deteriorate faster than almost any other fish. The flavoured salt used here makes a lovely fresh summery seasoning and any leftovers are great sprinkled over roasted vegetables or buttered potatoes or salads and vegetable dishes. A pot of mayonnaise, either plain or flavoured, or the Tomato Sauce in the Basic Recipes chapter, make delicious extras.

Serves 4

12–16 sardines, cleaned and gutted

15 ml (1 tablespoon) olive oil

FOR THE SALT

1 tablespoon coarse sea salt

1 teaspoon freshly ground black pepper

1 tablespoon finely chopped fresh thyme

1 garlic clove, peeled and crushed

finely grated rind of 1 lemon

10–12 fresh basil leaves, torn

Combine all the ingredients for the salt and decant into a small serving bowl.

Score the sardines several times along each side. Brush with the oil, and cook under a preheated grill (broiler), or use the barbecue or ridged pan, allowing 2–3 minutes each side, or until golden and cooked through.

Transfer to serving plates and serve with the salt for sprinkling.

red mullet with garlic bread sauce

∽

In some countries the guts and liver of red mullet are considered so tasty that the fish is cooked whole and the innards spread on toast or simply eaten with the fillets. If you find this a little too extreme for your taste ask the fishmonger to gut the fish for you, or do it yourself. You could try frying the livers in a little butter, but that is entirely up to you! This recipe has the delicious Mediterranean flavours of herb barbecued fish and bread sauce, inspired by the Greek recipe Scordalia.

Serves 4

4 red mullet, scaled and gutted

small bunch fresh thyme leaves

30 ml (2 tablespoons) olive oil

plenty of large sprigs of bay leaves

salt and freshly ground black pepper

FOR THE SAUCE

1 pitta bread, about 40 g (1½ oz)

a little milk for soaking

1 plump garlic clove, peeled and chopped

2 anchovy fillets, chopped

100 ml (3½ fl oz) olive oil

15–30 ml (1–2 tablespoons) white wine vinegar

Score the mullet several times along each side. Season the fish inside and out with salt and pepper and tuck several small bunches of thyme into the cavity of each. Brush the fish all over with olive oil.

To make the sauce, tear the bread into pieces and put in a bowl. Pour over enough milk to just cover, and leave to soak for 10 minutes. Lift out the bread, squeeze out and discard the excess milk, then put the bread in a food processor.

Add the garlic, anchovies and a dash of the oil and blend to a thick paste. Gradually blend in the remaining oil until the consistency slackens but remains quite thick. Blend in 15 ml (1 tablespoon) of the vinegar and test for seasoning (the sauce may be salty enough). Add a little more vinegar, if liked, for extra tang. Transfer to a serving dish.

Place the bay sprigs on the preheated barbecue and arrange the mullet on top. Cook for about 5 minutes on each side, or until cooked through. Alternatively, grill (broil) or cook the mullet in a ridged pan for a similar time. Serve with the sauce.

feta-stuffed squid

This recipe works best with squid tubes that are about 12 cm (4¾ in) long. Too small and they're fiddly to stuff, too big and they'll need a lot more stuffing and a longer cooking time. This is a good 'party' dish that you can prepare ahead of lighting up the barbecue.

Makes 12

45 ml (3 tablespoons) olive oil

1 onion, peeled and finely chopped

1 teaspoon fennel seeds

1 teaspoon cumin seeds

2 garlic cloves, peeled and crushed

200 g (7 oz) feta cheese

3 tablespoons finely chopped
    fresh coriander (cilantro)

3 tablespoons finely chopped fresh parsley

12 cleaned squid tubes

salt and freshly ground black pepper

Heat 15 ml (1 tablespoon) of the oil in a frying pan over medium heat. Add the onion and fry gently for 5 minutes.

Lightly crush the fennel and cumin using a pestle and mortar, or place them in a small bowl and use the end of a rolling pin to crush them. Tip the spices into the frying pan with the garlic, and fry for another minute. Remove from the heat, tip into a bowl and leave to go cold. Crumble in the feta, herbs and a little seasoning. Mix well.

Using a teaspoon pack the feta mixture into the squid tubes. This is a little fiddly and you might find it easier to use your fingers. Alternatively cut a small slit, about 1 cm (½ in) deep at the openings of the tubes so they're slightly wider to make stuffing easier. Refrigerate until ready to cook.

Soak 12 wooden skewers in hot water for 30 minutes. Thread a stuffed squid onto each by pushing the skewer up through the base of each tube and thread the closed ends at the other. Brush lightly with the remaining olive oil.

Cook on a preheated barbecue, or using a grill (broiler) or ridged frying pan. Allow 3–4 minutes on each side or until the squid has turned white and is lightly charred in places. Slice and serve.

haddock and caramelised
onion gratin

Haddock has a firm flaky flesh and plenty of flavour, which is complemented with a hearty caramelized onion topping. If you have a jar of caramelised onions or onion 'marmalade' in the cupboard use it instead of making your own for an even easier dish. Caramelised onions have a lovely sweet flavour that develops during long gentle frying. Serve with baby potatoes and a leafy salad or seasonal vegetables.

Serves 2

40g (1½ oz) butter

1 medium red onion, peeled and thinly sliced

2.5 ml (½ teaspoon) caster (superfine) sugar

15 ml (1 tablespoon) balsamic vinegar

5 ml (1 teaspoon) freshly chopped lemon thyme

2 haddock fillets, each weighing about 175–200 g (6–7 oz)

65 g (2½ oz) Gruyere cheese, grated (shredded)

finely chopped lemon thyme, to sprinkle

salt and freshly ground black pepper

To carmelise the onions, melt half the butter in a frying pan over a medium heat, add the onions and sugar, and cook very gently for about 8–10 minutes until very soft. Stir in the balsamic vinegar, lemon thyme and seasoning, and cook for another minute. Turn out onto a plate and wipe out the pan.

Melt the remaining butter in the pan and fry the haddock fillets briefly on each side for about a minute. Spoon the onion mixture over the top. Sprinkle with the cheese. Cook under a preheated grill (broiler) for 5–6 minutes or until the cheese is melting and bubbling.

chilli grilled sprats
with avocado mash

Sprats are so small that they're usually sold, cooked and served whole – heads and all! If this doesn't appeal then cut off the heads or gut them first, see Preparation Techniques.

Serves 4

700 g (1 lb 9 oz) sprats

1 teaspoon mild chilli powder

½ teaspoon ground coriander

½ teaspoon celery salt

1 tablespoon olive oil

FOR THE AVOCADO MASH

3 ripe tomatoes

2 ripe avocados

30 ml (2 tablespoons) lemon or lime juice

60 ml (4 tablespoons) sweet chilli sauce

1 small shallot, peeled and finely chopped

finely chopped fresh coriander (cilantro), to garnish

To make the avocado mash, pierce the tomato skins with a knife and place in a heatproof bowl. Cover with boiling water and leave for 1 minute or until the skins split. Drain, rinse in cold water and peel away the skins. Halve the tomatoes, scoop out and discard the seeds and dice the flesh.

Halve the avocados and scoop the flesh into a bowl. Mash well with a fork and add the lemon or lime juice, chilli sauce and chopped shallot. Mix well. Stir in the chopped tomatoes and turn into a serving dish.

Pat the fish dry on kitchen paper.

Put the chilli powder, coriander and celery salt in a very large plastic bag, and shake well to combine. Add the sprats and shake them around until coated in a thin dusting of spice.

Line a grill (broiler) rack with foil and brush lightly with the oil. Scatter the fish in a single layer and cook under a preheated grill for 2 minutes until the skin starts to crinkle and colour. Flip the fish over and cook for another 1–2 minutes. Serve with the avocado mash and a garnish of coriander.

chargrilled tuna with salmoriglio sauce

⁓

Tuna is the 'meatiest' type of fish and is cooked in the same way as beef steaks – rare, medium or cooked through depending on personal taste. If you have never tasted tuna when served pink in the centre, then it's worth trying it, as the texture is more tender and succulent. Cooked in a ridged pan, the fish will have appetisingly seared lines, or you could use a barbecue or conventional grill (broiler). The citrusy sauce is also delicious with kingfish steaks or whole grilled mackerel.

Serves 4

4 tuna steaks, about 2 cm (¾ in) thick
salt and freshly ground black pepper
30 ml (2 tablespoons) olive oil

FOR THE SALMORIGLIO SAUCE
2 tablespoons finely chopped fresh oregano

2 tablespoons finely chopped fresh parsley
3 garlic cloves, peeled and crushed
finely grated rind of 1 lemon, plus 30 ml
    (2 tablespoons) juice
2 teaspoons caster (superfine) sugar
120 ml (4 fl oz) olive oil

To make the salmoriglio sauce, put all the sauce ingredients in a screw-topped jar. Add a little salt and pepper and shake vigorously to blend.

Season the tuna steaks on both sides with salt and pepper and brush with the oil. Preheat a ridged pan, and cook the tuna steaks for 2 minutes. Turn the steaks and cook for another 1½ minutes for a steak that is still pink in the centre. For a very rare tuna steak cook for just 1 minute on each side, or for steaks that are cooked right through, allow 4–5 minutes each side.

Transfer the steaks to warmed serving plates. Shake the jar of dressing to mix the ingredients again, and spoon a little over each piece of fish. Serve the remainder in a small bowl.

grilled oysters

⁂

Seafood 'purists' eat oysters raw, directly from the half shell with a drizzle of lemon juice, Tabasco sauce or black pepper. If you would prefer to try them lightly cooked, then this recipe is perfect. Opening the oyster shells can be tricky, see Preparation Techniques for instructions.

Serves 2 as a snack or starter

12 oysters

50 g (2 oz) unsalted butter

2 shallots, peeled and finely chopped

1 garlic clove, peeled and crushed

15 ml (1 tablespoon) white wine vinegar

2 tablespoons finely chopped fresh parsley

freshly ground black pepper

Crumple a large sheet of kitchen foil onto a baking sheet. Shuck (open) the oysters using an oyster knife. Discard the top shell and run a knife under the oyster to loosen it from the lower shell. Place the oysters on the foil-lined baking sheet, nestling them in the foil so that they are supported enough to stop the juices escaping.

Melt the butter in a small frying pan and fry the shallots for 2–3 minutes until softened. Remove from the heat and stir in the garlic, vinegar, parsley and a little pepper. Stir together and spoon a little over each oyster. Cook under a preheated grill (broiler) for 2–3 minutes or until the oysters are just firm to the touch.

Transfer to serving plates and serve warm. To keep the oysters upright and prevent the juices running out, scatter plenty of coarse salt on a serving plate and push the oysters gently into the salt

grilled dab with chorizo butter

⚭

Dabs are smaller than plaice and sole and yield less meat to bone. A single dab is sufficient for a summery snack or light supper with a jacket potato or homemade chips to accompany. Flounder and small plaice can be cooked in the same way.

Serves 2

75 g (3 oz) unsalted butter, softened,
   plus extra to grease
2 dabs
salt and freshly ground black pepper
40 g (1½ oz) chorizo sausage, skinned
   and finely chopped

good pinch ground paprika
1 tablespoon finely chopped fresh
   coriander (cilantro)
1 spring onion (scallion), finely chopped
4 small plum tomatoes, quartered

Line a baking sheet with kitchen foil and grease generously with butter. Place the dabs on the foil, dark sides uppermost and season lightly with salt and pepper. Preheat the grill (broiler).

Put the butter and chorizo sausage in a food processor and blend until the ingredients form a reddish paste. Briefly blend in the paprika, coriander and spring onion and turn into a small serving dish.

Grill the dabs for 5 minutes then turn the fish over and scatter the tomatoes around the edges. Cook for another 3–4 minutes or until the fish is cooked through. Serve topped with the chorizo butter. (Freeze any leftover butter for topping any white fish, steamed vegetables or new potatoes.).

Indian-spiced salmon

These plump, marinated salmon fillets are easy to cook and look special. The fillets will cut into six generous portions, or serve narrower slices if you are barbecuing other fish or meats as well. If you are cooking using the grill (broiler) instead, turn it down to a lower heat once the surface of the fish is cooked. Serve with plain or spicy rice and thick yogurt, flavoured with a little lime juice and garlic.

Serves 6

2 x 600 g (1 lb 5 oz) middle-cut salmon fillets, skin on

15 cardamom pods

2 teaspoons cumin seeds

½ teaspoon ground cinnamon

20 g (¾ oz) piece fresh root ginger, grated (shredded)

1 red chilli, de-seeded and finely chopped

2 garlic cloves, peeled and crushed

30 ml (2 tablespoons) lemon or lime juice

30 ml (2 tablespoons) vegetable oil

25 g (1 oz) fresh coriander (cilantro), finely chopped, plus extra to garnish

salt

FOR THE YOGURT DRESSING

200 g (7 oz) Greek (strained plain) yogurt

1 garlic clove, crushed

squeeze of lime or lemon

Check the salmon fillets and remove any stray bones.

Crush the cardamom pods using a pestle and mortar, or place them in a small bowl and use the end of a rolling pin. Pick out the shells. Add the cumin seeds and pound the spices until coarsely crushed. Stir in the cinnamon, ginger, chilli, garlic, lemon juice, oil and coriander.

Spread the spice mixture over the salmon, except the skin, and place in a non-metallic bowl. Cover and chill for 1–2 hours.

Sprinkle the salmon with salt and transfer to a preheated barbecue, skin side down. Cook for 8–10 minutes, or until the skin is crisp and lightly charred. Turn the salmon over and cook for another 5 minutes, or until cooked through.

Make the dressing, combining all the ingredients in a small bowl.

Serve garnished with coriander.

barbecued fish with tahini sauce

Thin fillets of fish are easy to barbecue if you use a hinged fish grill, which makes them easy to turn. If cooking indoors use a ridged pan or a regular grill (broiler). Tahini paste is made from sesame seeds and gives sauces a delicious, nutty flavour.

Serves 4

2 teaspoons harissa paste

15 ml (1 tablespoon) olive oil

4 x 150 g (5 oz) firm fish fillets, such as bream
   or tilapia

50 g (2 oz) tahini paste

1 garlic clove, peeled and crushed

125 g (4 oz) Greek (strained plain) yogurt

15 ml (1 tablespoon) clear honey

25 g (1 oz) fresh parsley, roughly chopped

squeeze of lime or lemon juice, plus extra
   wedges to serve

4 pitta breads

2 small iceberg or little gem (bibb) lettuces,
   roughly sliced

Mix the harissa paste and olive oil together in a small bowl. Score each fish fillet several times along each side, and brush both sides with the oil mixture.

Put the tahini paste, garlic, yogurt and honey in a food processor and blend until smooth. Add the parsley and blend again until finely chopped and the sauce is specked green. Add a little lime or lemon juice to taste and transfer to a serving bowl.

Cook the fish on a preheated barbecue, or using a grill (broiler) or ridged frying pan. Allow 2–3 minutes on each side until the fish is cooked through.

Meanwhile, warm the pitta breads on the barbecue or in the oven preheated to 180°C/350°F/Gas Mark 4 for 5 minutes. Split open the pittas and tuck in plenty of lettuce, a piece of fish and a generous spoonful of the sauce. Serve with lime or lemon wedges.

Frying

Frying is one of the most popular ways to cook fish and it responds well to the process, sizzling to a crisp on the outside and staying moist and juicy in the centre. All fish can be fried, whether steaks, fillets, small whole fish or shellfish. Shallow-fry fish to cook it right through or to sear the surface and colour before finishing it in the oven or on the hob with other ingredients (such as in a stew). Deep-frying produces fabulous results – the fish is protected from the heat by a coating of batter or breadcrumbs, which cook to a crunchy crispiness. Stir-frying is a brilliant cooking method for shellfish or small pieces of fish. Cooked in minimal oil with additional ingredients such as vegetables and noodles, it provides a healthier, lighter way to cook.

Using the right type of cooking fat for frying is important. All fats have a different 'smoking point', meaning the temperature at which they start to smoke and break down. If heated beyond this the fat is likely to burn, turn bitter and taint the flavour of the finished dish. Vegetable oils such as groundnut, corn and sunflower have the highest smoking point and the least flavour. These are good for deep-frying. Vegetable oils and olive oil can be used for shallow-frying. Olive oil has a good flavour, though a lower smoking point, so you'll need to pay closer attention to the pan. Butter produces a lovely flavour but burns easily. You can reduce the risk of burning by adding a splash of vegetable oil to the frying pan when melting the butter. Unsalted butter is better than salted because it produces less sediment as it melts. 'Stir-fry' or 'wok' oils are usually groundnut oil flavoured with aromatic ingredients such as garlic and ginger, which add contributory flavours to Asian-style stir-fries. A regular vegetable oil can be used instead.

Shallow-frying

When shallow-frying have the pan hot before adding the fat or oil and then get this hot before adding the fish. If cooking small pieces, do not cram them too tightly in the pan – the lack of space will mean that the fish steams in its own juices rather than fries. The temperature of the oil will also be reduced so frying won't be as efficient.

In some shallow-fried fish dishes additional ingredients are added to the pan to make a sauce. If the pan has burnt specks of food around the edges lift out the fish, wipe out the pan and then complete the sauce. Cooking times will vary depending on the thickness and density of the fish so test that the fish is cooked through by piercing the thickest area of flesh with the tip of a knife.

Deep-frying

Although deep-fried fish tastes delicious, this is a potentially dangerous cooking method and extra care must be taken to prevent the oil from getting too hot. The safest way to deep-fry is to use an electric deep-fryer with a thermostat, in which the appliance turns off automatically if the oil gets too hot. A sturdy deep-frying pan with a frying basket can also be used, as well as a regular large pan. Fill the pan no more than one-third full with oil. Never leave the pan unattended and if possible use a thermometer to keep an eye on the temperature. For most deep-fried fish dishes the temperature should be 180–190°C (350–375°F), or until a piece of bread sizzles and turns golden in 1 minute. A large, wide pan, or a frying pan with deep sides filled with just 2 cm (½ in) of oil can also be used. This latter option is perfect for frying small whole fish or pieces of fish such as fish fingers with fresh mango chutney.

Stir-frying

Stir-fried fish dishes are fast to cook, delicious, and particularly suited to small pieces of firm-textured fish such as monkfish and salmon, shellfish such as scallops, prawns and lobster, or squid. Very little oil is needed for stir-frying as the ingredients get hot quickly and are constantly kept on the move by turning the ingredients with a spatula or spoon. Have all the ingredients chopped, and dressings, sauces and flavourings ready before you start. Fish and vegetables should be cut into small even-sized pieces so they cook quickly.

There are four basic steps to a simple stir-fry. First the aromatic flavourings such as shallots, garlic, chilli and ginger are cooked briefly in the hot oil to release their flavour. These are then drained while the fish is added to the flavoured oil and tossed around in the pan before removing this to a plate. The vegetables are added next, starting with the ones that take the longest to cook such as carrots and celery, gradually adding softer, faster cooking vegetables like courgettes (zucchini), mushrooms and spring onions (scallions). The ingredients should be kept on the move all the time. Finally, all the cooked ingredients are returned to the wok or pan along with any herbs, sauces or dressings, and noodles to heat through and combine. You can easily put together your own simple stir-fries using this basic method and any ingredients you have to hand, drizzling the finished stir-fry with a little light soy sauce, or ready made stir-fry sauce.

Frying tips

- A good quality pan is essential for successful frying, whether it's a heavy one for shallow-frying or a sturdy deep-fat fryer. They are expensive, but if properly looked after, will last many years.
- Always heat the pan properly before adding the oil or butter. Only add the fish once the butter is bubbling or the oil is hot. You'll notice that the consistency of the oil thins as it gets hot. If you try and fry in under-heated pans using warm, rather than hot oil, the fish will become soggy and frequently stick to the pan as it fries, particularly if you're using a pan that is not the best quality.
- Make sure the fish is thoroughly dry before frying. Moisture will cause spluttering and the fish will cook in steam created by the moisture. It will make a mess and never crisp up.
- For the simplest fried fish supper, score fish fillets and tuck wafer thin slices of garlic and a little chopped rosemary into the cuts. Season the fish on both sides and fry until crisp and cooked through. Delicious with a squeeze of lemon, peppery leaf salad, blob of mayonnaise and tasty bread.
- Because frying is such a quick form of cooking, have all your preparation done in advance. Accompaniments should be ready first and any ingredients and sauces used in a stir-fried dish should be ready to add to the wok.
- A large, sturdy fish slice is useful for removing or turning large fillets of fish or whole fish. Double length fish slices are available, which are large enough to slide under a whole fish to support it as it is transferred from pan to plate.
- When shallow-frying avoid the temptation to repeatedly turn the fish as it browns. A better colour and crisper skin will result if one side is browned completely before it is turned over, see crisping skin (opposite). The same applies to fishcakes and fish fingers.
- As a guide to shallow-frying times, allow about 2–3 minutes each side for a chunky fish fillet or cutlet, about 4 minutes per side for a small flat fish, and 5–6 minutes each side for a portion-sized round fish steak.
- Whether deep- or shallow-frying, don't put too much fish in the pan at once because it will reduce the temperature of the oil and the fish won't fry to a crisp.
- Have a plate covered with several layers of kitchen paper ready to transfer deep-fried fish onto. The paper will soak up the excess oil and help keep the coating crisp.
- If the oven is not in use, set it to a low temperature and use it to keep cooked fish warm when frying fish. This is particularly useful if you are deep-frying in batches.
- Oil that's been used for deep-frying fish can be used one or twice more. Leave it to cool completely before straining it through a fine sieve (strainer) into a jug (pitcher). Pour back into the bottle and store in a cool place (clearly labelled that the oil has been used for frying fish). When discarding used oil, pour it into an oil bottle or similar carton and put out with the kitchen waste rather than pouring it down the sink.

Crisping fish skin

The skin of most white fish, as well as salmon, crisps well. Try this simple skill and you'll be adding flavour, texture and visual appeal to your dish. Make sure the fish has been properly scaled before cooking, as the scales will not soften during frying, and will look unsightly and taste awful. Cut the fish into portions if not already done and pat dry on kitchen paper. Season both sides of the fish with salt and pepper. (A generous amount of salt on the skin side will help crisp and add flavour to the skin.) Heat a little oil, or mixture of butter and oil, in a good quality frying pan. Once hot, add a couple of fish fillets to the pan, skin side down and fry for several minutes until you can see the flesh turning opaque around the edges and the skin looks deep golden and crisp. Press the fish down firmly with a fish slice (or base of a thoroughly clean pan if frying several pieces) to create maximum contact for even crisping. This will also stop the fish curling up in the heat of the oil. Once the fillets are crisped, turn them over to cook the flesh sides, either right through for serving, or very lightly if you're finishing the dish in another way, for example braising.

Coating fish in breadcrumbs

Plain (all-purpose) flour, beaten egg and breadcrumbs are three basic coatings that work together to give fried dishes such as fish fingers their irresistibly crunchy coating. It is a simple technique (though possibly slightly messy!) and can be done in advance of frying so all your preparation is complete.

Tip a little flour onto a plate and season with salt and pepper. Beat an egg in a bowl, and on another plate sprinkle breadcrumbs. (Crushed spices or chopped herbs can be added to the breadcrumbs if you're feeling adventurous.) Take several pieces of prepared fish and turn lightly in the flour until dusted on all sides using your hands. Lift from the flour, shaking off the excess and add to the beaten egg. Turn the fish in the egg until coated then lift out, letting the excess egg drip back onto the plate. Place on the breadcrumbs and turn the fish until coated. Transfer to a clean plate or board while you coat the remaining pieces of fish. (You can make the task less messy by using one hand to do the 'dry' coatings and one to do the 'wet'.)

family fishcakes

Any inexpensive white fish is great for fishcakes, particularly when it's combined with other well-flavoured ingredients. In this case, it's a cheese and spring onion-flavour mash.

Serves 4

400 g (14 oz) floury potatoes, peeled and chopped
  into chunks
450 g (1 lb) white fish fillets, such as coley
  or whiting
60 ml (4 tablespoons) milk
75 g (3 oz) Gruyère cheese, grated
25 g (1 oz) butter
1 bunch spring onions (scallions), chopped

1 egg yolk
finely grated rind of 1 lemon
salt and freshly ground black pepper
flour, for dusting
vegetable oil, for frying
lemon wedges, seasonal vegetables or salad,
  mayonnaise or ketchup, to serve

Cook the potatoes in plenty of lightly salted boiling water until they're just tender, about 15 minutes.

Meanwhile put the fish in a frying pan, add the milk and cover with a lid. Cook gently for 8–10 minutes until cooked through. Discard the milk, and transfer the fish to a plate until cool enough to handle.

Drain the potatoes and return to the pan. Mash the potatoes, they needn't be completely smooth, and stir in the cheese.

Melt the butter in a clean frying pan and fry the spring onions for 1 minute. Tip into the potato pan with any juices.

Flake the fish into small pieces, discarding the skin and any bones. Add to the potato pan with the egg yolk and lemon rind Stir well to combine but so that the fish stays in chunky pieces. Season with pepper and a little salt, if needed.

Divide the mixture into four even amounts. Using lightly floured hands, shape into balls and flatten into cakes about 2 cm (¾ in) thick. Heat a thin layer of oil in a clean frying pan and gently fry the cakes for about 3 minutes on each side until golden. Serve hot with lemon wedges, seasonal vegetables or salad, mayonnaise or ketchup.

beer-battered fish with chunky chips

Homemade fish and chips are so easy – the trick is being organised so that everything is ready to serve at the same time. See beginning of the chapter for deep-frying information before you start. In this version, beer and baking powder make the batter light, while turmeric adds a golden colour. Serve with Crushed Minted Peas, see Basic Recipes chapter.

Serves 4

50 g (2 oz) plain (all-purpose) flour,
   plus extra for coating
50 g (2 oz) cornflour (cornstarch)
½ teaspoon baking powder
¼ teaspoon ground turmeric
salt and freshly ground black pepper
150 ml (¼ pint) beer

4 x 175–200 g (6–7 oz) fillets of white fish such as
   pollack, haddock or cod, skinned
vegetable oil, for deep frying
750 g (1 lb 10 oz) potatoes, for chipping, such as
   Maris Piper
lemon or lime wedges, to serve

Put the flours, baking powder and turmeric in a bowl and add a little salt and pepper. Mix well, then make a well in the centre of the bowl and pour in half the beer. Whisk gently using a balloon whisk, blending the ingredients until the mixture forms a paste. Gradually whisk in the remaining beer, then leave the batter to stand for 1 hour.

Remove any stray bones from the fish and pat dry on kitchen paper. Season a little flour on a plate with salt and pepper and use to lightly coat the fish.

Cut the potatoes lengthways into slices about 1.5 cm (5/8 in) thick. Cut across into chunky chips and place in a bowl of cold water until ready to cook. Drain the potatoes, then pat dry between several layers of kitchen paper.

Fill a deep-fat frying pan or large, heavy pan with oil and heat to 180–190°C (350–375°F) or until a cube of bread sizzles and turns golden in 1 minute. Lower half the potatoes into the pan (preferably in a frying basket). Fry for about 5 minutes until the chips turn pale golden. Drain, then transfer to a plate lined with kitchen paper while you part-cook the remainder in the same way.

Dip a piece of fish in the batter, let the excess run back into the bowl and lower the fish into the oil. Do the same with another piece of fish. (You'll may only fit two pieces of fish in the oil at the same time so you'll need to cook in batches.) Cook the fish for about 4–5 minutes until crisp and golden, transferring to a kitchen paper-lined plate to drain while you cook the remainder. Keep warm.

Return the chips to the hot oil and fry for a few minutes to crisp up. Drain on kitchen paper and serve with the fish and lemon or lime wedges.

paella

There are many regional versions of this classic Spanish dish. This recipe combines plenty of authentic flavours creating a fabulous dish you can always rely on. The secret is to use a generous amount of olive oil, which will absorb all the fishy, meaty flavours, which are then transferred to the rice as it gently swells up. Use bone-in or ready-boned chicken or rabbit portions. Boneless are easier to eat though the bones do provide extra flavour

Serves 4

2 tomatoes

120 ml (4 fl oz) olive oil

4 small chicken thighs or rabbit portions

8 large raw prawns, peeled and de-veined

350 g (12 oz) squid, cleaned and sliced into rings

120 g (4½ oz) chorizo, finely diced

1 red (bell) pepper, de-seeded and diced

1 onion, chopped

6 garlic cloves, crushed

½ teaspoon mild paprika

250 g (9 oz) Paella rice

1 teaspoon saffron strands

500 ml (18 fl oz) fish or chicken stock

200 g (7 oz) fresh mussels, cleaned

salt and freshly ground black pepper

lemon wedges, to serve

Pierce the skin of each tomato with a sharp knife and place in a heatproof bowl. Cover with boiling water and leave for 1 minute or until the skins split. Drain, rinse in cold water and peel away the skins. Chop the tomatoes into small pieces.

Heat half the oil in a large frying pan or paella pan. Add the chicken or rabbit and fry gently, turning the pieces until they start to colour. Push to one side and add the prawns and squid to the pan. Fry gently for a couple of minutes, turning the prawns to colour both sides. Using a slotted spoon, drain the meat and fish and put on a plate.

Add the remaining oil to the pan and heat through. Stir in the chorizo and cook gently for 5 minutes until the oil turns golden. Drain and add to the plate.

Add the red pepper and onion to the pan and fry gently for a few minutes until softened. Stir in the tomatoes, garlic and paprika, and cook for another minute. Tip in the rice and turn it in the oil until coated. Crumble the saffron over the rice.

Push the chicken pieces into the rice and add the stock. Bring to the boil and reduce the heat to its lowest setting. Cook gently for 20–25 minutes without stirring until the rice is just cooked through.

Add the squid, prawns and mussels, pushing them down into the rice with a wooden spoon. Cover with a lid or foil and cook for another 4–5 minutes or until the mussels have opened. (Discard any mussels that do not open.) Leave to stand for 10 minutes before serving with lemon wedges.

prawn tempura with dipping sauce

Tempura batter is lighter than a fish and chip batter and should be used immediately while very cold. This recipe makes the perfect starter or light supper dish when served with salad.

Serves 4

16–20 large raw prawns, peeled and de-veined,

1 egg yolk

100 ml (3½ fl oz) chilled sparkling water

40 g (1½ oz) plain (all-purpose) flour, plus extra
    for coating

vegetable oil, for deep frying

salt and freshly ground black pepper

FOR THE DIPPING SAUCE

15 ml (1 tablespoon) wasabi paste, optional

30 ml (2 tablespoons) dark soy sauce

30 ml (2 tablespoons) Japanese mirin

1 hot red chilli pepper, deseeded and finely chopped

Place a prawn on a board and open out so that the underside faces upwards. Make several shallow diagonal cuts into the prawn with a sharp knife. This isn't an essential step but it helps to prevent the prawns from curling up as they cook. Repeat with the remainder. Season a little extra flour with salt and pepper on a plate. Turn the prawns in the flour to coat and shake off the excess. Chill until ready to cook.

To make the sauce, put the wasabi paste in a bowl and gradually beat in the soy sauce, mirin and chilli. Turn into a small serving dish.

Heat a 5 cm (2 in) depth of oil in a wok or deep-sided frying pan to 190°C (375°F). While the oil is heating, beat the egg yolk in a bowl with the water. Add the flour all in one go and whisk with a balloon whisk until the batter is mixed. (It need not be completely smooth.)

Check that the oil has reached the specified temperature. If you don't have a thermometer, the oil is ready when a cube of bread sizzles on the surface and turns golden in 1 minute. Take one quarter of the prawns and dip each into the batter one at a time. Hold each at the tail end and carefully lower them into the oil. Cook for about 90 seconds until pale golden. Transfer with a slotted spoon to a plate lined with kitchen paper and keep warm while you cook the remainder. Serve with the dipping sauce.

fried squid rings with chilli tomato salsa

This delicious summery dish is best when made with medium-sized squid tubes that are about 12–16 cm (4¾–6¼ in) long. Too small and they'll fry too quickly, too large and they may be tough. Sweet chilli sauce, mixed with diced tomato, spring onion and coriander makes a really easy salsa.

Serves 4

400 g (14 oz) squid tubes, cleaned and cut into 1 cm
   (½ in) thick slices

plain (all-purpose) flour, for dusting

vegetable oil, for deep frying

salt and freshly ground black pepper

FOR THE SALSA

4 ripe tomatoes

45 ml (3 tablespoons) sweet chilli sauce

1 spring onion (scallion), finely chopped

15 ml (1 tablespoon) finely chopped fresh coriander
   (cilantro), plus extra to garnish

Pat the squid rings dry on kitchen paper.

To make the salsa, halve the tomatoes, scoop out and discard the seeds. Finely dice the flesh and mix with the sweet chilli sauce, spring onion and coriander. Transfer to a small serving dish.

Pour a 5 cm (2 in) depth of oil into a large pan, deep-sided frying pan or deep-fat fryer. Heat to 180–190°C (350–375°F), or until a piece of bread sizzles and turns golden in 1 minute. Sift the flour onto a plate and season with plenty of salt and pepper.

Add about a third of the squid rings to the flour and mix with your hands until thoroughly coated. Lift from the flour and carefully lower into the oil. Cook for 1–2 minutes or until golden. Drain with a slotted spoon and place on a plate lined with kitchen paper while you cook the remainder in batches. Serve with the salsa.

American crab cakes

These crab cakes resemble fishcakes but are much spicier and are flavoured with peppers and onions instead of mash. Make them ahead of time and chill for several hours, or overnight, so that all that's left to do is the frying.

Serves 6

15 ml (1 tablespoon) vegetable oil, plus
    extra for frying

1 red onion, chopped

2 red (bell) peppers, deseeded and chopped

30 ml (2 tablespoons) mayonnaise

5 ml (1 teaspoon) Dijon mustard

1 teaspoon mild chilli powder

1 medium egg, beaten

45 ml (3 tablespoons) finely chopped fresh parsley

300 g (11 oz) mixed brown and white crabmeat

120 g (4½ oz) breadcrumbs

salt

flour, for dusting

Mayonnaise or Fresh Tomato Sauce, see
    Basic Recipes

lemon wedges and salad leaves, to serve

Heat the oil in a frying pan over a medium heat. Add the onion and peppers and fry gently for about 10 minutes until tender and golden. Tip into a large bowl and leave to cool.

Add the mayonnaise, mustard, chilli powder, egg, parsley, crabmeat and breadcrumbs to the bowl. Stir well until the ingredients are evenly combined. Check the seasoning, adding a little salt if necessary.

Turn the mixture out onto a lightly floured surface and divide into six even portions. Shape each into a ball and flatten into a cake.

Heat a thin layer of oil in a frying pan and fry the cakes for 2–3 minutes on each side until golden. Serve with mayonnaise or tomato sauce, lemon wedges and salad leaves.

peppered brill fillets

This is such an easy recipe to make and is cooked in a similar way to classic 'steak au poivre'. It works well with almost any firm-textured fish including salmon, tuna, kingfish and halibut.

Serves 2

2 chunky brill fillets, skin on, each about
   200 g (7 oz)
2 teaspoons freshly ground coarse black pepper
salt
15 ml (1 tablespoon) vegetable oil

15 g (½ oz) butter
2 shallots, peeled and finely chopped
150 ml (¼ pint) fish stock
60 ml (4 tablespoons) double (heavy) cream

Pat the pieces of brill dry on kitchen paper. Mix the ground black pepper with a little salt and press all over the skinless sides of the fish.

Heat the oil with the butter in a frying pan until bubbling. Add the shallots and fry gently for 3 minutes until tender. Push the shallots to one side, then add the brill to the pan, skin sides down, and cook for about 4 minutes or until the skin is crisp and golden and the fish is opaque almost through to the centre.

Turn the fish with a fish slice and cook gently for another 3 minutes until the thickest area of the fish is cooked through.

Drain the fish and place on warmed serving plates. Add the fish stock to the pan. Bring to the boil and let the mixture bubble and reduce by about half. Stir in the cream and return to the boil. Season to taste, and spoon over the fish to serve.

scallop, bacon and samphire salad

This recipe demonstrates how easy it can be to turn out an impressive 'cheffy'-looking starter. Have your dressing and ingredients prepared ahead and then the cooking is easy. If you buy huge, meaty scallops allow just one per serving and increase the frying time to one minute each side.

Serves

18 medium-sized scallops with roes

75 g (3 oz) thin-cut rashers (strips) of smoked streaky (fatty) bacon

200 g (7 oz) samphire

15 ml (1 tablespoon) mild olive oil

25 g (1 oz) butter

FOR THE DRESSING

finely grated rind and juice of 2 lemons

75 ml (5 tablespoons) mild olive oil

30–45ml (2–3 tablespoons) white wine vinegar

40 g (1½ oz) caster (superfine) sugar

5 ml (1 teaspoon) Dijon mustard

1 garlic clove, peeled and crushed

1 tablespoon lemon thyme, freshly chopped

To make the dressing, put all the dressing ingredients in a large screw-topped jar and shake well to mix.

Pat the scallops dry on kitchen paper. Cut each bacon rasher into three pieces.

Discard any woody stalk ends from the samphire and rinse in several changes of cold water. Drain well. Bring a pan of water to the boil. Tip in the samphire and return to the boil. Cook for 1 minute, then drain through a colander and rest over the pan while you start frying.

Heat the oil in a frying pan and fry the bacon until golden and crisp. Lift out onto a plate and keep warm. Add the butter to the pan and heat until bubbling. Reduce the heat and add the scallops. Cook for 30 seconds until turning pale golden on the underside then turn over and cook for another 30 seconds. Drain on a kitchen paper-lined plate.

Pile the samphire onto warmed serving plates and arrange the scallops and bacon on top. Shake the dressing ingredients in the jar to combine and spoon over and around the salad to serve.

fish fingers with fresh mango chutney

These homemade fish fingers are a thousand times better than bought, frozen ones. This version uses a cornmeal coating, and the accompanying fruity sauce gives a slightly Caribbean flavour. For a more conventional approach, use breadcrumbs or coarse oatmeal for coating and serve with tomato sauce.

Serves 4

500 g (1¼ lb) firm, chunky white fish fillets, skinned and any stray bones removed

2 tablespoons plain (all-purpose) flour

salt and freshly ground black pepper

1 egg

100 g (3½ oz) cornmeal (cornstarch)

vegetable oil for frying

FOR THE CHUTNEY

1 large, ripe mango

½ medium-strength red chilli, de-seeded and finely chopped

1 shallot, finely chopped

finely grated rind of 1 lime, plus 15 ml (1 tablespoon) juice

1 tablespoon caster (superfine) sugar

To make the chutney, slice the mango on each side of the flat central stone (pit). Cut away the skin and flesh from around the stone. Finely chop all the flesh and put in a small pan with any juices on the board. Add the chilli, shallot, lime rind and juice, sugar and 30 ml (2 tablespoons) water.

Cook gently, uncovered, for 10 minutes, stirring frequently and adding a dash more water if the mixture starts to dry out. Once soft and pulpy tip the chutney into a bowl and leave to cool.

Cut the fish fillets across into 1 cm (½ in) thick slices. Sprinkle the flour onto a plate and add a little salt and pepper. Beat the egg to break it up in a shallow bowl. Sprinkle the cornmeal on another plate.

Lightly dust each piece of fish in seasoned flour then dip in the egg. Let the excess drip back onto the plate, then roll the fish fingers in the cornmeal until coated.

Heat a thin layer of oil in a large frying pan. Add half the fish, spacing them well apart and fry for about 2 minutes or until the undersides are golden. Turn the pieces carefully and cook for another minute or until cooked through. Transfer to a plate lined with kitchen paper and cook the remainder, adding a dash more oil to the pan if it has run dry. Serve with the chutney.

stir-fried prawns with noodles

Prawns are great for stir-frying as they can be tossed around in the pan without falling apart. Always take care not to overcook them as they'll turn rubbery and will shrivel.

Serves 4

250 g (9 oz) rice noodles

400 g (14 oz) raw peeled prawns, de-veined

60 ml (4 tablespoons) chunky peanut butter

150 ml (¼ pint) hot fish stock

45 ml (3 tablespoons) dark soy sauce

30 ml (2 tablespoons) rice wine vinegar

15 ml (1 tablespoon) Thai fish sauce

1 tablespoon light muscovado (brown) sugar

60 ml (4 tablespoons) wok or stir-fry oil

4 garlic cloves, peeled and thinly sliced

20 g (¾ oz) piece fresh root ginger, grated (shredded)

150 g (5 oz) mangetout (snowpeas), halved lengthways

1 bunch spring onions (scallions), trimmed and sliced

65 g (2 ½ oz) cashew nuts

Cook the rice noodles following the instructions on the packet. (This is usually done by cooking them briefly in boiling water or putting them in a heatproof bowl and covering with boiling water to soften.) As soon as they've softened but retain a little texture drain them from the water, bearing in mind that they'll soften further in their own heat.

Pat the prawns dry on kitchen paper.

Put the peanut butter in a small bowl and blend in the stock, soy sauce, vinegar, fish sauce and sugar.

Heat half the oil in a large frying pan or wok and add the garlic and ginger. Stir-fry for 1 minute, then drain the ingredients and put on a plate with a slotted spoon. Add the prawns to the pan and fry, stirring for about 2 minutes until they've turned pink, by which time they'll be cooked through. Lift out onto the plate.

Heat the remaining oil in the pan and add the mangetout. Stir-fry for 1 minute then add the spring onions and cashew nuts and cook for another minute.

Return the prawns to the pan with the garlic and ginger, drained noodles and peanut butter mixture. Cook, stirring for a couple of minutes until the ingredients are heated through. Serve immediately.

stir-fried monkfish
with mushrooms

ঞ৩

Firm-textured monkfish holds together well as it cooks, making a perfect choice for stir-frying. Coconut
cream is a richer form of coconut milk though the milk can be used instead.

Serves 4

500 g (1¼ lb) monkfish fillet

1 teaspoon cornflour (cornstarch)

60 ml (4 tablespoons) vegetable or wok oil

3 garlic cloves, peeled and chopped

25 g (1 oz) fresh root ginger, grated (shredded)

1 hot red chilli, de-seeded and thinly sliced

5 ml (1 teaspoon) cumin seeds, crushed

1 stalk lemongrass, chopped

1 small onion, peeled and thinly sliced

200 g (7 oz) shitake mushrooms, thinly sliced

150 ml (¼ pint) coconut cream

25 g (1 oz) fresh coriander (cilantro),
    finely chopped

salt and freshly ground black pepper

seamed basmati or Thai rice, to serve

Prepare the monkfish, and cut into 1 cm (½ in) thick slices. (If you're using a very chunky
piece of fillet, cut it in half lengthways first.) Pat the fish dry on kitchen paper. Season the
cornflour with salt and pepper and use to dust the fish.

Heat half the oil in a large frying pan or wok and add the garlic, ginger, chilli and cumin.
Stir-fry for 1 minute then drain the ingredients to a plate with a slotted spoon. Add the
monkfish to the pan and fry, stirring for about 2 minutes until the fish has turned completely
white. Drain then remove to a plate lined with kitchen paper.

Heat the remaining oil in the pan and add the lemongrass and onion. Cook, stirring for
3 minutes until the onion starts to soften. Stir in the mushrooms and cook for another
2–3 minutes until starting to colour.

Return the garlic, spices and fish to the pan with the coconut, coriander and 45 ml
(3 tablespoons) water. Heat through for 1–2 minutes. Serve on a bed of rice.

Stewing, braising and poaching

Stewing, braising and poaching share a common link in that they're all moist forms of cooking in which the fish is immersed totally or partially in liquid. The liquid might be water, stock, wine, alcohol, tomato juice or even olive oil. Not only does the liquid flavour the fish, but the fish gives its flavour to the liquid resulting in a delicious, juicy dish that saves you the trouble of making an accompanying sauce. Other flavouring ingredients such as vegetables, beans, lentils, herbs and spices can also be added for flavour, and texture. Whole fish can be cooked using any of these methods: whole poached salmon being a classic example. For fuss-free family eating or easy entertaining, however, it is easiest to use filleted fish, which can be served straight from the dish and it doesn't matter so much if it breaks up. Fish is usually added to the pot raw, the exception being crisped skin fillets used in the braised mullet with mushrooms and cabbage recipe. When using other ingredients such as vegetables, herbs and spices in a recipe, cook these before adding the fish so they have time to soften and their flavours meld together.

Stewing

Fish stews, flavoured with plenty of vegetables, garlic, herbs, spices and tomatoes are a popular dish in Mediterranean countries, where a feast of different fish, including small, whole ones that are too small to fillet, are combined in one delicious pot in which the fish and bones flavour the juices. Ladled into bowls, sometimes over slices of bread, and topped with aioli, they make a fabulous dish at any time of year. The recipe on page 00 is a simple version using filleted fish and fish stock so you don't have to fiddle with small fish and bones. Once you've made a couple of fish stews, it's so easy to experiment with your own recipe ideas. Think of flavours that go together such as tomatoes with Mediterranean herbs, coconut milk with Indian spices or sweet-sour Asian blends, and create your own dishes. There are no rules about proportions of ingredients – as long as the dish has a soupy, stew-like consistency and the fish is not overcooked, you'll be amazed by the results. Fish cooked in this way is fabulous 'one pot' food that can be served simply with bread for mopping up the juices, or for a more substantial meal with a dish of creamy mash, polenta, couscous, rice or ribbon pasta.

Braising

Fish braises are made by nestling pieces of fish or whole fish on a partially cooked 'base' of ingredients that include vegetables, pulses, herbs or spices in a well-flavoured liquid. They are usually covered with a lid and baked in the oven or on the hob. Occasionally the fish might be fried first to impregnate flavour, or seared to crisp the skin, in which case it will be braised without a lid. Braised dishes are great for any occasion from everyday comfort food to entertaining friends.

Poaching

Poaching is a no-fuss, easy way to cook fish and can be a light and healthy choice too. The well-seasoned, flavoured stock in which the fish is cooked can be used as the base for a delicious sauce retaining the goodness and flavour that has developed as the fish has cooked. You can either serve the poached fish in its liquid, or drain the fish and keep it warm while you reduce the liquid for the base of a sauce.

Stewing, braising and poaching tips

- This is the chapter where homemade fish stocks play a useful and delicious role. Make stock using bones saved from preparing fish (or that the fishmonger has supplied). Bought stock can also be used. A good quality stock cube is acceptable for everyday eating.
- All fish, except strongly flavoured oily ones, are good for these cooking methods.
- Use the correct-sized pans or casserole dishes for stewing and poaching. Too small and the contents will be bubbling over the top, too large and the fish won't be sufficiently submerged in liquid. A medium-sized, double-handled flameproof pan with lid is a useful piece of equipment. You can use it on the hob or in the oven and take it to the table for serving. A deep-sided (and not too large) roasting pan is good for braising as it's easy to nestle the pieces of fish into the vegetables and juices. Use kitchen foil to cover the pan in place of a lid, if necessary.
- For 'special occasion' cooking, prepare the dish to the step before adding the fish. Have the fish trimmed and ready to pop in so all you need do is reheat it before adding the fish.
- Keep an eye on the dish as it cooks. If it's cooked on the hob with a lid, check frequently that the liquid is not bubbling away furiously as the fish will overcook and break up. The liquid should be barely moving. If you cannot reduce the heat low enough move the pan to one side of the hob plate.
- When fish is immersed in liquid it cooks more quickly than 'dry'-cooked fish. Bear this in mind if you're making any salads or vegetable accompaniments so you can have these ready first.
- Avoid the temptation to stir fish stews as they cook. The fish is more likely to fall apart.
- For an easy poached fish supper, lightly cook smoked haddock, cod or pollack in milk and serve topped with a poached egg or on a bed of wilted spinach, topped with a cheese or parsley sauce made using the poaching liquid.
- Check the seasoning of the dish before serving as the flavours will have mingled and developed. You might find it needs a little more salt and pepper though often the flavours are salty enough. Much depends on the stock used.
- Fish dishes do not need to 'rest' like meat, but stews and soups usually benefit from standing for 10 minutes before serving so they're not too hot for the flavours to be appreciated.

creamy white fish, tarragon and cauliflower soup

⤶⤷

Use any white fish, including a mixture of fillets , if you like, for this flavour-packed soup. It is cooked briefly in a herby, mildly spiced stock before blending to a smooth consistency. Serve small portions as a starter or in larger bowl with chunks of crusty bread for a main course.

Serves 6–8

450 g (1 lb) white fish fillets, such as haddock, pollack, cod, whiting, skinned

50 g (2 oz) butter

1 onion, peeled and sliced

2 sticks celery, sliced

1 litre (1¾ pints) fish stock

1.25 ml (¼ teaspoon) ground allspice

1 small cauliflower, cut into small florets

400 g (14 oz) can butter (lima) beans or cannellini beans, rinsed and drained

several long sprigs of tarragon

200 g (7 oz) green beans, stalks removed, and cut in half

150 ml (¼ pint) single (light) cream

salt and freshly ground black pepper

Cut the fish into small chunks, discarding any stray bones.

Melt half the butter in a large pan and add the onion and celery. Cook gently, stirring frequently, for 5 minutes until the onion has softened.

Add the fish stock, ground allspice, cauliflower florets and butter or cannellini beans, and bring just to the boil. Reduce the heat to its lowest setting, cover and cook gently for 15 minutes until the cauliflower is soft. Pull the tarragon leaves from their stalks. Add half to the pan. Lower in the fish and cook gently, covered for another 5 minutes.

Melt the remaining butter in a small pan, add the French beans and turn in the butter. Add a teaspoon of water and the remaining tarragon, cover and cook gently for 8–10 minutes, stirring the beans occasionally until just tender.

Using a stick blender, or by blending in batches in a food processor, blend the soup until completely smooth. Return to the rinsed-out pan and stir in the cream with a little seasoning to taste. Ladle the soup into bowls and pile the beans and any juices on top.

Serve with basmati rice or warmed flatbreads.

fish molee

This is a classic fish curry cooked in coconut from Kerala in Southern India. It is spicy and aromatic but not fiery hot. The spices are fried first before the fish is added to release and blend the flavours. Have all the ingredients chopped and ready to hand before you start cooking – the rest is easy.

Serves 4

700 g (1 lb 9 oz) chunky white fish fillets, such as cod, pollack, coley or monkfish, skinned

½ teaspoon salt

1.25 ml (¼ teaspoon) ground turmeric

3 tomatoes

60 ml (4 tablespoons) vegetable oil

2 teaspoons yellow mustard seeds

½ teaspoon fenugreek seeds

2 teaspoons ground coriander

1 medium strength green chilli, de-seeded and finely chopped

3 shallots, peeled and sliced

4 garlic cloves, peeled and crushed

25 g (1 oz) piece fresh root ginger, grated (shredded)

400 ml (14 fl oz) can coconut milk

salt and freshly ground black pepper

Check the fish and remove any stray bones. Cut into chunky pieces, roughly 5 cm (2 in) across. Pat the fish dry on kitchen paper. Mix together the salt and turmeric and sprinkle over the fish.

Pierce the skin of each tomato with a knife and place them in a heatproof bowl. Cover with boiling water and leave for 1 minute or until the skins split. Drain, rinse in cold water and peel away the skins. Chop the flesh.

Heat 45 ml (3 tablespoons) of the oil in a large pan or flameproof casserole and add the mustard and fenugreek seeds. Fry very gently until the seeds just start to crackle and pop. Stir in the coriander, chilli and shallots and fry gently for another 3 minutes. Add the garlic and ginger and fry for 2 minutes. Push the ingredients to one side of the pan.

Add the remaining oil to the pan, heat, and add the fish. Fry gently for 2 minutes, turning the fish until opaque, 3–4 minutes. Remove the fish and set aside on a plate.

Pour the coconut milk into the pan with the spice and bring to a simmer. Cover and cook gently for 10 minutes. Add the tomatoes to the pan along with the fish then cook for another 10 minutes. Season to taste.

stewing, braising and poaching

Mediterranean fish stew

The ingredients list for this recipe may be long but the cooking method couldn't be more straightforward. It's simply a case of methodically adding the ingredients and building up a delicious 'one pot' meal. The easiest accompaniment is warmed ciabatta, though a bed of polenta, or rice, would also be good.

Serves 5–6

800 g (1 lb 12 oz) mixed white fish fillets such as halibut, brill, monkfish, bream, gurnard or mullet, skinned

60 ml (4 tablespoons) olive oil

1 large onion, peeled and chopped

2 celery sticks, scrubbed and chopped

2 red (bell) peppers, de-seeded and roughly chopped

5 garlic cloves, peeled and crushed

3 pared strips orange zest

2 x 400 g (14 oz) cans chopped tomatoes

10 ml (2 teaspoons) caster (superfine) sugar

60 ml (4 tablespoons) sun-dried tomato paste

500 ml (18 fl oz) fish stock

1 teaspoon saffron threads

50 g (2 oz) pitted black olives

250 g (9 oz) squid rings

250–300 g (9–11 oz) mussels or clams, prepared

salt and freshly ground black pepper

Garlic Mayonnaise, optional, see Basic Recipes

Check the fish and remove any stray bones. Cut the fillets into chunky pieces, about 5 cm (2 in) across. Season with salt and pepper.

Heat the olive oil in a large heavy pan. Add the onion and fry gently for 5 minutes. Add the celery and red peppers and fry gently for another 10 minutes, until the vegetables are lightly coloured, stirring frequently. Add the garlic and orange rind and fry for another 2 minutes.

Add the tomatoes, sugar, tomato paste and fish stock. Crumble in the saffron strands and bring the stew to a gentle simmer. Cook gently, uncovered, for 15 minutes.

Add the thickest pieces of fish to the stew. Reduce the heat to its lowest setting and cook for 5 minutes, then add the thinner pieces of fish, olives, and squid rings. Put the mussels or clams on top. Cover with a lid or foil. Cook for another 5 minutes, or until the shells have opened up.

Ladle into large bowls, discarding any mussel or clam shells that remain closed. Serve with Garlic Mayonnaise for spooning onto the stew, if you like.

monkfish tagine

Spicy Moroccan stews offer a gentle method of cooking fish, allowing it to absorb all the delicious flavours of the North African spices. A 'tagine', meaning the vessel the stew is cooked in, is traditionally used over a stove or open fire and has a conical lid with a vent in the top to allow steam to escape. If you have a tagine that you wish to use to serve the dish, but are not sure whether it is suitable for using over a modern hob, start the stew in a frying pan and transfer to the tagine for oven cooking at 180°C/350°F/Gas Mark 4 for 25 minutes. Serve with warmed flatbreads or steamed couscous.

Serves 4

15 g (½ oz) fresh coriander (cilantro)

2 garlic cloves, peeled and roughly chopped

1 medium strength red chilli, deseeded and
    roughly chopped

good pinch of saffron threads

2 teaspoons ras el hanout spice blend

30 ml (2 tablespoons) sun-dried tomato paste

700 g (1 lb 9 oz) monkfish fillet, prepared

45 ml (3 tablespoons) olive oil

1 large fennel bulb, chopped

1 onion, chopped

200 ml (7 fl oz) fish stock

2 preserved lemons

salt and freshly ground black pepper

Roughly cut the bunch of coriander into shorter sprigs including stalks and put in a food processor with the garlic, chilli, saffron, spice blend and tomato paste. Blend to a thick, coarse paste, scraping down any mixture from the sides of the bowl.

Cut the monkfish into 3–4 cm (1¼–1½ in) chunks and put in a bowl. Add the paste and mix with the fish until well coated. Cover loosely and chill for about an hour.

Heat the oil in a tagine or flameproof casserole. Add the fennel and onion and fry gently for 6–8 minutes until softened. Tip in the coated fish and cook gently, slowly turning the fish for 5 minutes. Add the stock and bring to a very gentle simmer. Cover with a lid or foil and cook on the lowest heat for 20 minutes.

Halve the preserved lemons, scoop out the pulp and discard. Finely chop the flesh and stir into the tagine. Check the seasoning for taste.

braised fish with lentils, anchovies and tomatoes

Cooking fish on a well-flavoured bed of garlicky lentils and tomatoes gives you a complete dish with plenty of juiciness. It is substantial enough to serve on its own, or you may wish to offer a bowl of buttery mash or seasonal vegetables with it.

Serves 4

150 g (5 oz) Puy lentils

60 ml (4 tablespoons) olive oil

1 onion, peeled and finely chopped

6 garlic cloves, peeled and halved lengthways

2 teaspoons finely chopped fresh rosemary

400 g (14 oz) can chopped tomatoes

2 teaspoons light muscovado (brown) sugar

150 ml (¼ pint) fish stock

4 tablespoons finely chopped fresh parsley

50 g (2 oz) can anchovies, or 6 fillets, chopped

8 white fish fillets, such as haddock, whiting, pollack, cod, skinned and boned, roughly 650 g (1 lb 7 oz) total weight

salt and freshly ground black pepper

Rinse the lentils in a sieve (strainer) and tip into a medium pan. Cover with plenty of cold water and bring to the boil over medium-high heat. Reduce the heat and simmer gently for 15 minutes or until almost tender. Strain.

Preheat the oven to 180°C/350°F/Gas Mark 4. Heat 45 ml (3 tablespoons) of the oil in a large pan or flameproof casserole and gently fry the onion for 6–8 minutes until lightly browned. Add the garlic and rosemary and cook for another 2 minutes.

Stir in the tomatoes, sugar and fish stock and bring to the boil. Cover with a lid and transfer to the oven for 30 minutes until the garlic cloves have softened.

Stir the parsley and anchovies into the lentils and season with salt and pepper. Nestle the fish down into the lentils and drizzle the fish with the remaining oil. Cover and cook for another 20 minutes, or until the fish is cooked through.

braised mullet with mushrooms and cabbage

လၢ

Before braising in the oven, these fish skins are fried to a crisp and are used to add flavour to the dish. This is also really good with any bream or bass.

Serves 4

1 small savoy cabbage

650 g (1 lb 7 oz) grey mullet fillet, boned and cut into portions

60 ml (4 tablespoons) olive oil

3 shallots, peeled and finely sliced

250 g (9 oz) mushrooms, cleaned and thinly sliced

1 teaspoon caraway seeds

200 ml (7 fl oz) fish stock

150 ml (¼ pint) dry white wine

100 ml (3½ fl oz) crème fraîche

salt and freshly ground black pepper

Preheat the oven to 180°C/350°F/Gas Mark 4. To prepare the cabbage, discard any damaged outer leaves, then pull away any loose green leaves and cut away the thick stalks. Roll up the leaves and slice across them to shred as finely as possible. Quarter the white part of the cabbage and slice off and discard the cores. Slice this as thinly as possible.

Pat the fish dry on kitchen paper and season on both sides with salt and pepper. Heat 15 ml (1 tablespoon) of the oil in a large frying pan. Add the fish fillets, skin sides down and fry until crispy. Turn the fillets over and fry the flesh sides for 30 seconds. Remove from the pan with a fish slice and place on a plate.

Heat the remaining oil in the pan and gently fry the shallots for 3 minutes. Add the mushrooms and cook until beginning to brown and the juices have evaporated. Stir in the cabbage and caraway seeds and toss the ingredients together over the heat for 2 minutes.

Tip the cabbage and mushroom mixture into a large, shallow ovenproof dish or roasting pan. Add the fish stock, wine and crème fraîche to the frying pan and bring to the boil. Arrange the fish portions on top, skin sides face up and nestling the fillets down into the cabbage. Bake, uncovered for 20 minutes, or until the fish is cooked through.

bacon-stuffed bream with leeks

Black bream s firm fleshed, sweet and perfect for sandwiching around a tasty filling. Pink bream and gilt head bread can also be used successfully or, failing their availability, use fillets of sea bas.

Serves 4

4 medium leeks

50 g (2 oz) butter

5 ml (1 teaspoon) ground coriander

250 ml (8 fl oz) fish stock

75 g (3 oz) smoked streaky (fatty) bacon, diced

2 shallots, finely chopped

2 garlic cloves, peeled and finely chopped

75 g (3 oz) breadcrumbs

4 tablespoons finely chopped fresh parsley

4 black bream fillets

100 g (3½ oz) peas, fresh or frozen

salt and freshly ground black pepper

Preheat the oven to 180°C/350°F/Gas Mark 4. Trim the leeks discarding any tough outer layers and wash well. Cut diagonally into chunky slices, about 3–4 cm (1¼–1½ in) across.

Melt half the butter in a frying pan over medium heat and gently fry the leeks for about 5 minutes, stirring frequently. Add the coriander, stock and some salt and pepper. Tip into a shallow ovenproof dish or flameproof casserole, cover with a lid or foil and transfer to the oven for 20 minutes.

While baking, heat a frying pan and dry-fry the bacon for 3–4 minutes until it starts to crisp. Add the shallots and garlic and fry for another 2 minutes. Tip the ingredients into a bowl and melt the remaining butter in the heat of the pan. Stir in the breadcrumbs and parsley, stirring to coat in the butter. Add to the bowl and season with plenty of black pepper. Leave to cool.

Arrange two bream fillets, skin sides down on the work surface and pack the stuffing mixture on top. Stack the remaining fillets on top, skin sides uppermost. Tie string around each fillet sandwich to hold the pieces together then slice through the centre of each so you have four portions.

Stir the peas into the leeks and add the bream portions, pushing them down into the vegetables. Cover and return to the oven for another 25 minutes or until the fish is cooked through.

cockle and prawn risotto

ᔓᔓ

Shellfish such as mussels, clams and cockles are usually steamed open in a pan with a scant amount of liquid. In this recipe, the cockles are cooked gently in stock in a similar way to poaching. This method cooks the cockles and creates a hot, flavourful stock – one of the main components of a good risotto. You could use cooked prawns instead of raw, but only add them for a minute to heat through or they'll start to toughen.

Serves 4

2 celery sticks, roughly chopped

3 bay leaves

2 onions, peeled, 1 chopped, 1 quartered

1 kg (2 ¼ lb) cockles in their shells, prepared,

25 g (1 oz) butter

2 garlic cloves, finely chopped

300 g (10 oz) risotto rice

150 ml (¼ pint) dry white wine

4 tablespoons finely chopped fresh parsley

100g (3½ oz) mascarpone

150g (5oz) raw peeled prawns, de-veined if large

salt and freshly ground black pepper

Put the celery, bay leaves and quartered onion in a large pan with 1 litre (1¾ pints) water and bring to the boil. Reduce the heat to a gentle simmer and cook gently for 15 minutes. Tip in the cockles. Cook gently for another 5 minutes until the cockles open. Using a slotted spoon transfer the cockles to a large bowl. Discard the vegetables and bay leaf, but reserve the cooking liquid in the pan.

Once the cockles are cool enough to handle, remove three-quarters of the clams from their shells, discarding any that are damaged or failed to open. Bring the stock to a gentle simmer.

In a large pan, over medium heat melt the butter and add the chopped onion. Cook gently for 5 minutes until softened. Add the garlic and rice, and stir for 2 minutes. Pour in the wine and cook, stirring until the wine has evaporated, about 2 minutes. Add a ladleful of the stock and stir until the liquid has mostly evaporated. Continue to cook the risotto, stirring continuously and adding a ladleful of stock every few minutes until the consistency turns thick and creamy. The risotto is ready once all, or most of the stock has been used and the rice grains are soft but retaining a little bite.

Stir in the parsley, mascarpone, shelled and unshelled cockles and prawns, and mix well. Heat through for a few minutes to cook the prawns and check the seasoning before serving.

poached sole with herbs, capers and olives

Poach fish in a well-flavoured liquid, infused with herbs and garlic and you'll have a delicious 'ready made' sauce that is full of flavour and goodness. Serve with rice or buttered new potatoes.

Serves 4

fillets of 2 large lemon sole, skinned

3 shallots, peeled and halved

15 g (½ oz) fresh parsley, remove and retain the stalks, finely chop the leaves

3 bay leaves

2 lemon slices

1 plump garlic clove, peeled and finely chopped

2 tablespoons capers, rinsed, drained and chopped

10 pitted black or green olives, roughly chopped

45 ml (3 tablespoons) double (heavy) cream

salt and freshly ground black pepper

Season the fish with salt and pepper, then fold each fillet in half to make a neat, compact shape.

Put the shallots in a large frying pan. (Choose one in which the folded fish will fit quite compactly in a single layer.) Add the parsley stalks to the pan with the bay leaves, lemon slices and garlic. Add 500 ml (17 fl oz) water and bring to the boil. Reduce the heat to a gentle simmer and cover with a lid. Cook gently for 20 minutes.

Add the fish to the pan and adjust the heat so the liquid is barely moving. Cover and cook very gently for 6–8 minutes, or until the fillets are cooked through. Carefully transfer the fish to serving plates using a slotted spoon and keep warm.

Bring the pan juices to the boil and boil for 5–6 minutes, or until the mixture is reduced by about two-thirds (150 ml/¼ pint, if measured). Strain and return the liquid to the pan. Stir in the chopped parsley, capers, olives and cream, and season to taste with salt and pepper. Spoon over the fish, to serve.

olive oil-poached fish with artichoke and bean salad

This is a lovely way to cook fish, particularly if you're going to serve it with a fresh, colourful Mediterranean-style salad. Use a casserole dish in which the fish fits quite snugly so you don't have to use too much oil. This recipe also works well using salmon fillets.

Serves 4

4 x 150–175g (5–6 oz) pieces tuna or kingfish steak

1 tablespoon sea salt

1 teaspoon ground paprika

6 garlic cloves, peeled and thinly sliced

several sprigs of thyme

4 limes, thinly sliced

approximately 250 ml (8 fl oz) olive oil

300 g (10 oz) baby broad (fava) beans

150 g (5 oz) chargrilled artichoke hearts from a tub or deli counter

150 g (5 oz) chargrilled red or mixed (bell) peppers (in a jar)

½ small red onion, peeled and thinly sliced

25 g (1 oz) mixed fresh coriander (cilantro), parsley and mint, finely chopped, plus extra to garnish

Preheat the oven to 150°C/300°F/Gas Mark 2. Sprinkle the fish on both sides with the salt and leave to stand for 15 minutes. Rub off the excess seasoning with kitchen paper. (There's no need to be too thorough with this). Sprinkle the fish all over with the paprika.

Drizzle a little oil over the base of a wide, shallow ovenproof casserole, or ovenproof frying pan in which the fish fits quite snugly in a single layer. Arrange the fish in the dish and tuck the garlic and thyme around it. Arrange the lime slices on top and pour over the oil so the fish is just covered.

Cover with a lid and poach in the oven for 20–22 minutes or until the fish has turned opaque. The centre of the fish will still be pink in the centre, so if you prefer it cooked through, continue poaching for an extra 10 minutes.

Meanwhile, put the broad beans in a pan and cover with boiling water. Cook over medium heat for 5 minutes then drain and tip into a bowl. (If there is time, peel the pale outer skins away from some of the beans to reveal the deep emerald colour, which looks stunning).

Cut the artichokes and peppers into small pieces and add to the bowl of beans along with the onion and herbs. Mix well and season lightly.

To serve, pile the salad onto serving plates. Lift the fish out of the oil with a fish slice and place on top of the salads. Drizzle a little of the cooking oil on top and scatter with a few of the lime slices and extra herbs.

Steaming and microwaving

Steaming is the gentlest way to cook fish. The fish retains maximum flavour and keeps its shape perfectly as steam circulates freely around it. For this reason it is also seen as a 'forgiving' cooking method – an extra couple of minutes in the steamer will not overcook or dry out fish as it might with other methods of cooking. Steaming is used for whole fish, fillets, cutlets and shellfish. Delicate fish types respond well to steaming as they are less likely to fall apart. Adding oil or butter is optional so steaming fish can be an incredibly healthy way to cook. Prior to cooking fish can be rubbed with spices, garlic or herbs; it can be stuffed with aromatic ingredients, or the cooked ingredient can be served with an array of tempting sauces. The wealth of fabulous Asian steamed-fish dishes clearly illustrate that there's nothing dull about steamed fish! You can even steam fish in the oven using a wire rack and roasting pan. Shellfish, particularly mussels, clams and cockles are also very good steamed. What is more delicious than a steaming bowl of mussels, laced with garlic, herbs and cream.

For serious cooks, microwaves can play a useful role in the kitchen. A plain piece of fish seasoned and dotted with butter can be cooked in the microwave and will develop the same texture and flavour as one that is steamed. White fish or salmon fillets will cook to a moist and succulent texture, perfect for blanketing in a creamy sauce, serving alongside a crunchy salad, or flaking into a pie or kedgeree dish. Don't forget the microwave is handy for speedily thawing fish you've forgotten to remove from the freezer!

Utensils for steaming

There are several different types of steamers available to buy. Whichever you use, the steaming rack for fish should be at least 3 cm (1¼ in) above the liquid level.

- For steaming one or two portions of fish, a collapsible metal fan steamer (sometimes called a lotus steamer) that fits into a pan is ideal.
- Asian bamboo steamers are available in many sizes and can be rested over a pan or inside a wok. Smaller ones will only accommodate small pieces of fish, or rolled fillets, while larger ones can take whole fish.
- Traditional pan steamers have a metal steamer with slotted bases that fit inside a large pan. These can accommodate several portions of fish.
- A small round wire rack (the type used for cooling cakes) can be rested over a wok or frying pan and covered with a lid or tent of kitchen foil to trap the steam. Some woks have steamer racks that fit inside the wok and can be covered with a wok lid or kitchen foil.

- For oven-steaming, use a roasting pan and small wire rack that fits inside the pan. If the legs of the rack are less than 2 cm (¾ in) deep, raise the rack on individual metal pudding basins, one in each corner.
- Free-standing electric steamers are also widely available and you'll need to refer to appliance instructions for usage. They vary considerably in price and offer many different features such as digital timers and delayed start options. Only buy one if you really enjoy this style of cooking or risk it getting relegated to the back of the cupboard!

How to steam fish

Prepare the fish following your chosen recipe. Fit the steamer rack over the pan and pour boiling water into the pan – allow up to about a 5 cm (2 in) depth of water (or a 1–2 cm/½–¾ in) depth if oven-steaming. Ensure the water level is sufficiently lower than the rack on which the fish will be positioned. Arrange the fish on the rack, spacing the pieces apart slightly if steaming portions. Cover with a lid or foil so all the steam will be trapped inside. Turn the heat to a low setting and cook the fish. After cooking, take care when lifting the lid as the steam will be very hot. Lift the lid away from you. If using a foil 'lid', make sure your hands are behind the foil when unwrapping.

The method for steaming shellfish is slightly different in that they are plunged directly into a large pan containing a small amount of hot wine, stock or water. When covered with a lid the steam quickly accumulates and forces the shells to open. This usually only takes about 5 minutes and once the shells have opened the fish is cooked. Shake the pan several times during steaming to loosen the shells and encourage opening.

How to microwave fish

Portion-sized fish fillets or cutlets are ideal for microwaving. Make sure you use a microwave-proof dish and lightly brush it with oil before adding the fish so it doesn't stick. Arrange the fish in a single layer, leaving a space between the pieces. If microwaving fillets or pieces of fish with thin tail ends, arrange the pieces so the thinner areas overlap in the centre of as the outer edges will be first to cook, then the fish will cook evenly. Season lightly with salt and pepper. Herbs and spices can be tucked around the fish as you would when steaming. Brush with olive oil or dot with butter, if liked, and cover with cling film (plastic wrap), leaving a small corner uncovered so the excess steam can escape. Microwave at full power allowing about 4–5 minutes per 500 g (1¼ lb) for chunky fillets, or 3–4 minutes per 500 g (1¼ lb) for whole or filleted small flat fish. Take care when removing the cling film as the steam inside will be very hot. Leave to stand for 5 minutes before serving.

Tips for steaming and microwaving

• Dishes and bowls that get hot while the fish stays warm are not ideal for microwaving. You can test whether a container is suitable by microwaving it with a little water. If the container gets hot while the water is slow to heat up then it won't be suitable for cooking.

• If you're thawing fish in the microwave, arrange the pieces in the same way as if you were cooking them, see above, and cover with cling film. Microwave on the Defrost or Low setting, allowing 5–6 minutes for each 500 g (1¼ lb) fish. If the pieces are in a frozen block that you cannot separate, microwave briefly and separate the pieces as soon as they've softened enough. Check the fish every couple of minutes, turning and re-arranging them if some areas are starting to cook while others remain frozen.

• Shellfish such as prawns, scallops and crabmeat defrost very quickly. After the first minute of defrosting, keep checking every 30 seconds, turning and re-arranging the shellfish where possible. Squid will take a little longer but again, keep an eye on it, checking that some areas aren't starting to cook.

• Be aware that microwaving continues slightly once the dish is removed from the oven. If the fish is fractionally undercooked when you test it, leave it in its dish, covered with cling film and it'll finish cooking through.

• Don't pack fish too tightly together in the steamer. Leave at least a 1 cm (½ in) space between the pieces so the steam can circulate.

• If steaming whole fish, remove the heads if steamer space is a bit tight.

• Steaming times will vary according to the type of steamer used and how much fish you're steaming. As a guide, a whole, small flat fish and small rolled fillets will take about 8–10 minutes, a chunky fish portion will take about 12 minutes, and a large rolled fillet will take 12–15 minutes.

• Use a large pan or stockpot for steaming mussels or clams. They need plenty of room to swell up as they open. Ideally they shouldn't come more than about half way up the pan when you tip them in.

red mullet with Asian salad

If you prefer, use fillets instead of whole fish, allowing two per portion. Hot horseradish sauce can be used instead of wasabi paste.

Serves 4

1 small fennel bulb

2 carrots

½ bunch spring onions (scallions),
    trimmed and sliced

400 g (14 oz) pak choi (bok choy), finely shredded

25 g (1 oz) fresh coriander (cilantro),
    finely chopped

30 ml (2 tablespoons) chilli-infused oil

15 ml (1 tablespoon) vegetable oil

salt

4 small red mullet, gutted and scaled

FOR THE DRESSING

40 g (1½ oz) caster (superfine) sugar

30 ml (2 tablespoons) white wine vinegar

60 ml (4 tablespoons) vegetable oil

30 ml (2 tablespoons) light soy sauce

15 ml (1 tablespoon) lime juice

10 ml (2 teaspoons) wasabi paste

Slice the top off the fennel and remove any coarse or damaged outer layers. Slice the fennel as thinly as possible.

Cut the carrots into 5 cm (2 in) batons. Slice these lengthways as thinly as possible, then cut the lengths into thin matchsticks. Mix the fennel, carrots, spring onions, pak choi and coriander in a salad bowl. Drizzle with 15 ml (1 tablespoon) of the chilli-infused oil, all of the vegetable oil and a little salt.

Remove the fish heads if they will fit more easily in the steamer without them. Score down each side and brush with the remaining chilli oil. Sprinkle lightly with salt. Steam for 12 minutes or until cooked through.

To make the dressing, put the sugar in a small pan with 60 ml (4 tablespoons) water. Heat gently until the sugar dissolves. Raise the heat a little and cook until the syrup reduces slightly and thickens. Pour into a bowl and mix in the wine vinegar, vegetable oil, soy sauce, lime juice and wasabi paste.

Pile the salad and fish onto serving plates. Spoon over the dressing and serve.

steamed plaice with soy greens

Rolled fillets of small flat fish look pretty and hold their shape well during steaming. This recipe is easy to make as well as healthy — great for midweek eating. Serve with rice or rice noodles.

Serves 2

fillets from 1 large plaice

2 spring onions (scallions), trimmed and
    finely chopped

3 tablespoons finely chopped fresh
    coriander (cilantro)

150 g (5 oz) purple sprouting broccoli

45 ml (3 tablespoons) dark soy sauce

15 ml (1 tablespoon) clear honey

200 g (7 oz) spinach, tough stalks removed

freshly ground black pepper

If you have 'double' fillets, where the two fillets from each side of the fish remain intact, split them into single fillets. Skin the fillets. Lightly season with salt and pepper.

Mix together the spring onions and coriander and spread down the length of each fillet. Roll up the fillets starting from the thin ends. (If the fillets unravel secure them in place with wooden cocktail sticks).

Cut each broccoli stem in half lengthways and steam for 5 minutes until just tender. Remove from the steamer and add the rolled plaice fillets. Cover and steam for about 15 minutes until cooked through.

Meanwhile, mix the soy sauce with the honey and a little pepper in a small bowl.

Put the spinach in a large pan and drizzle with 15 ml (1 tablespoon) water (unless the spinach has just been washed, in which case there's no need to add any water). Cover with a lid and cook for 1–2 minutes until wilted but not completely soft. Add the broccoli florets and mix together.

Pile the vegetables onto warmed serving plates and arrange the fish on top. Drizzle with the dressing and serve.

sea bass with peanut and herb dressing

Like all other white fish, sea bass steams beautifully. If the fillets do not fit in a single layer in the steamer, fold them, or cut each into two pieces. The fish is simply steamed with a spice rub and brought to life with a tasty, crunchy topping.

Serves 2

2 x 150 g (5 oz) sea bass fillets

½ teaspoon ras el hanout spice blend

1 garlic clove, peeled and crushed

finely grated rind and juice of 1 lime

25 g (1 oz) salted peanuts, chopped

10 g (¼ oz) fresh parsley, finely chopped

several mint leaves, chopped

3 dates or 1 tablespoon raisins, chopped

15 ml (1 tablespoon) clear honey

15 ml (1 tablespoon) olive oil

salt and freshly ground black pepper

rice or couscous, to serve

Check the sea bass and remove any stray bones Score the fillets diagonally.

Mix the spice blend with the garlic, lime rind and a little salt and pepper and rub over the fish. Place in the steamer and cook for 10–12 minutes or until cooked through.

Meanwhile, put the peanuts, herbs, and dates or raisins in a bowl and add the lime juice, honey and olive oil.

Transfer the fish to warmed serving plates and spoon over the dressing. Serve with rice or couscous.

oven-steamed salmon
with chilli vierge

Vierge is a garlicky herb sauce that's lovely with salmon, and equally good with trout. The sauce can be made while the fish is cooking, or in advance and reheated. Oven-steaming is a great way of cooking, keeping all the steam hidden away!

Serves 4

4 salmon fillets, skin on, or cutlets, each weighing about 175 g (6 oz)

salt

FOR THE SAUCE

4 tomatoes

100 ml (3 ½ fl oz) extra virgin olive oil

1 medium strength red chilli, de-seeded and finely chopped

½ teaspoon ground cumin

15 g (½ oz) fresh herbs, such as chervil, parsley, tarragon, chives, finely chopped

1 garlic clove, peeled and crushed

finely grated rind and juice of 1 lime

Preheat the oven to 180°C/350°F/Gas Mark 4. Rest a wire rack inside a roasting pan.

Season the salmon lightly with salt and space the portions slightly apart on the wire rack and place over the cooking pan. Take a large piece of foil and cover the tin like a tent, making sure you leave space around the fish. Scrunch the foil around the top of the pan to hold it in place, but leave one corner unsealed for adding the water.

Pour 500 ml (18 fl oz) boiling water into the pan, seal the foil and bake the fish for 25 minutes. Carefully remove from the oven, unwrap a corner of the foil and check that the fish is cooked. If necessary, return it to the oven for a few more minutes.

To make the sauce, pierce the skin of each tomato with a knife and place in a heatproof bowl. Cover with boiling water and leave for 1 minute or until the skins split. Drain, rinse in cold water and peel away the skins. Halve the tomatoes, scoop out and discard the seeds. Chop the flesh into small dice.

Put the olive oil in a pan with the chilli and cumin. Heat through gently for a couple of minutes until the spices are just beginning to sizzle. Remove from the heat and stir in the tomatoes, herbs, garlic, lime rind and juice and a little salt.

Transfer the fish to serving plates and spoon over the sauce.

clam and tomato linguini

Use small clams such as palourdes for this recipe. Combined with the tomatoes, wine, onion and garlic, they make a delicious and robust sauce for pasta.

Serves 4

1 kg (2¼ lb) small fresh clams

150 ml (¼ pint) dry white wine

60 ml (4 tablespoons) olive oil

1 large onion, finely chopped

2 garlic cloves, peeled and crushed

800 g (1¾ lb) can plum tomatoes

45 ml (3 tablespoons) sun-dried tomato paste

1 teaspoon caster (superfine) sugar

300 g (11 oz) fresh linguine or 250 g (9 oz) dried

20 g (¾ oz) fresh parsley, finely chopped, plus extra, to sprinkle

salt and freshly ground black pepper

Prepare the clams. Pour the wine into a large pan and bring to the boil. Tip in the clams and cover with a lid. Cook for about 5 minutes, shaking the pan frequently until the shells have opened. Tip the clams and wine into a colander resting over a bowl to catch the juices. Leave to cool.

Clean the pan and heat the olive oil. Add the onion and fry gently for 5 minutes until softened. Add the garlic and fry for another minute. Tip in the tomatoes, tomato paste, sugar and clam cooking juices. Bring to the boil. Reduce the heat slightly and cook, uncovered until the sauce is thickened and pulpy, stirring frequently, about 15 minutes.

Meanwhile, bring a large pan of salted water to the boil. Lower in the linguine and bring to the boil. Cook fresh pasta for about 2–3 minutes and dried for 8–10 minutes (or follow the packet instructions).

Remove half the clams from the shells and discard any shells that remain closed. Add all the clams to the sauce with the parsley. Season to taste with salt and pepper.

Drain and return the cooked pasta to the pan. Add the sauce, mix well and pile onto serving plates, garnished with parsley.

garlic mussels

What is more delicious than a bowl of hot steaming mussels, drenched in deliciously creamy juices. Mop up the juices with homemade chunky oven chips, or some warmed fresh bread for the perfect accompaniments. The chips should be almost ready when you start to cook the mussels – you can always turn the oven right down so that chips and mussels are ready to serve at the same time.

Serves 2–3 as a main course, or 4 as a starter

1 kg (2 ¼ lb) fresh mussels

50 g (2 oz) butter

1 small fennel bulb, finely chopped

4 garlic cloves, peeled crushed

15 ml (1 tablespoon) plain (all-purpose) flour

150 ml (¼ pint) dry white wine

2 tablespoons finely chopped fresh parsley

2 tablespoons finely chopped fresh tarragon

60 ml (4 tablespoons) crème fraîche

salt and freshly ground black pepper

Prepare the mussels. Melt the butter in a large pan. Add the fennel and fry gently for about 5 minutes to soften. Add the garlic and fry for another minute. Tip in the flour and cook, stirring for 1 minute. Gradually blend in the wine, stirring well to remove any lumps. Bring the mixture to the boil.

   Tip in the mussels and cover with a lid. Cook for about 5 minutes, shaking the pan frequently until the shells have opened. Using a slotted spoon drain the mussels and transfer to warmed serving dishes. Add the herbs and crème fraîche to the juices in the pan and bring to the boil, stirring. Season to taste and pour over the mussels to serve.

clam chowder

᭤᭤

Clams vary in size from the small vongole variety favoured in Italy, to the larger carpet shell or palourdes, even larger quahog clams and long slender razor clams. All can be used in this recipe, though you'll need to increase the quantity by about a third if using very small clams, as the ratio of meat to shell is smaller. Serve as a hearty starter or in larger portions as a main course with chunks of bread.

Serves 4

1 kg (2¼ lb) clams, cleaned

25 g (1 oz) butter

150 g (5 oz) streaky (fatty) bacon, chopped

1 large onion, chopped

3 bay leaves

15 ml (1 tablespoon) plain (all-purpose) flour

200 g (7 oz) can chopped tomatoes

300 g (11 oz) potatoes, roughly diced

3 tablespoons finely chopped fresh parsley

5–10 ml (1–2 teaspoons) Tabasco sauce

60 ml (4 tablespoons) crème fraîche

salt

Bring 150 ml (¼ pint) water to the boil in a large pan. Tip in the clams and cover with a lid. Steam for about 5 minutes, shaking the pan frequently until the clams have opened. Drain through a colander resting over a bowl to catch the juices. Leave to cool.

Melt the butter in a clean pan and gently fry the bacon, onion and bay leaves, stirring frequently for 6–8 minutes until the bacon starts to colour. Add the flour and cook stirring for another minute.

Remove from the heat and blend in the clam cooking juice and 450 ml (¾ pint) water. Stir in the tomatoes, potatoes and parsley and bring to the boil. Reduce the heat to its lowest setting, cover with a lid and cook gently for 20 minutes.

Remove the clams from their shells, discarding any that remain closed. If using large clams or razors chop them into smaller pieces. Add to the pan with the Tabasco sauce and crème fraîche and cook gently for 5 minutes until heated through.

Sever the chowder as a chunky soup, or if you prefer, partially blend it using a hand blender or by lightly whizzing in the food processor. Season to taste with a little salt, if needed, and reheat before serving.

Raw, cured and smoked

This chapter is a miscellany of recipes that use smoked fish, fish that's cured with salt or pickling ingredients, and a couple of recipes in which fish is served raw. Before the days of refrigeration, fish was smoked or pickled (and sometimes salted and dried) so that it could be preserved and eaten all year round. Now we can enjoy these ways of preparing fish purely for their taste and texture, which can be quite different to conventionally cooked fish.

Raw fish

Eating raw fish has been popular in some cultures for as long as most of us have eaten it cooked. Japanese chefs spend years perfecting the choosing, preparation and suitable flavourings for Suchimi, their raw fish dishes. The appeal of eating raw fish is its absolute, unspoilt freshness and lingering scent of the sea, enhanced only by the simplest dressings or accompaniments. The difficulty for many of us – particularly if we don't live near a market, good local supplier or go fishing – is finding fish that's fresh out of the sea, which is vital for eating raw. This is not only an issue of flavour but safety, as parasites will thrive in aged fish or ones that has not been stored properly. Only ever buy fish for eating raw from a very good fishmonger whose counter displays the quality of fish described is extremely high. Prepare and eat the fish on the day you buy it.

Cured fish

In its simplest form, curing is done by rubbing salt, or a mixture of salt, sugar and other aromatic ingredients into a piece of fish to extract moisture and therefore intensify the flavour and firm up the texture. Chefs like to 'semi-cure' fish like this, sometimes simply for an hour or two so that the seasoning can seep right into the fish before being rinsed off and the fish cooked. The delicious Indian gravad lax on page 00 takes this method one stage further. By blanketing the fish in salt, sugar and spices and weighting it for a couple of days, the flavour of the fish is intensified, sweetened and spiced. It takes on the texture of smoked salmon (though is less oily) and is so easy to make, even for first-time cooks. Another way of serving fish without actually cooking it is to use lemon juice or vinegar. When fish is steeped in, or drizzled with, an acidic ingredient, the texture and colour of the fish changes and it takes on a cooked appearance. Many different cuisines still use this way of preparing fish, often called 'escabeche'. The acidic ingredient is often sweetened, flavoured with aromatic ingredients and poured over raw or lightly fried fish.

Smoked fish

Since ancient times we have smoked our food to protect it and keep it safe to eat. Now we smoke food because it tastes so good. The smoked fish we buy is first cured by steeping it in salt or brine to extract moisture (and therefore inhibit deterioration) before hot or cold smoking. Most hot-smoked fish such as mackerel and salmon require no further cooking as the fish is smoked at high temperatures, therefore cooking it at the same time. Cold-smoked fish is smoked through an indirect smoke supply in which there is no heat. This usually does need cooking as in the case of smoked haddock and cod.

Tips for cured and smoked fish

• Smoked fish will store in the refrigerator for a slightly longer time than fresh fish. Store on a plate or in a dish and lightly cover with greaseproof paper, baking parchment, or plastic wrap. It also freezes well.

• Some cheap mass produced versions are injected with chemically flavoured brine and given an artificial glaze to mimick a naturally smoked appearance. The surface of the fish is often a deep yellow colour. The fish might receive minimal smoking, if any at all.

• The undyed fish is considered superior because it's undergone a natural smoking process so there's no need for added colour or artificial flavourings. Hence, the flavour will also be better.

• Oily fish smokes very well, as its natural oil quickly absorbs smoky flavours. As oily fish naturally deteriorates at a faster rate than non-oily fish, the process of smoking increases its shelf life. Many oily fish, from sprats to mackerel, are readily available smoked, and provide an economical and tasty meal.

• Delicatessens and supermarkets often sell cured fish ranging from rollmops (pickled herrings) to soused (vinegar and herb-marinated) mackerel. These are relatively expensive to purchase, considering the cost of the raw ingredients, so may be worth making them yourself from scratch. It's also very easy.

Tips for preparing raw fish for eating

• Make sure all of your equipment, for instance, chopping board, knife and plate and scrupulously clean before you start. If you're preparing a whole fish, including scaling, gutting, filleting and skinning, thoroughly clean the board and knife once all the messy work is done.

• Once prepared, dip the cleaned fillets or pieces of fish in chilled salted water and pat dry on kitchen paper before slicing up the fish.

• Raw fish is usually eaten in very thin slices. Use a sharp knife and cut thin slanting slices from the fillet so that you're cutting against the 'grain' of the fish. By cutting across the grain you're cutting through the muscles and cartilage that hold the fish together therefore making the pieces more tender. Use this method for preparing gravadlax too.

• Fish 'carpaccio' is an Italian way of serving raw fish. The fish is sliced as thinly as possible, arranged in a single layer and drizzled with olive oil, herbs, capers and seasoning. It's delicious with sea trout.

• Halibut, sea bass, salmon, tuna and scallops are great favourites for serving raw.

indian-style gravad lax

This recipe is ideal if you are looking for a special starter to serve to a large crowd. It is easy to prepare and is made in advance. This is an Indian-style gravad lax because Indian spices take the place of the dill and pepper used in a traditional Swedish recipe. Gravad lax makes delicious finger food, or canapés, when served as a topping on toasted rye bread, with a drizzle of garlic sauce on top.

Serves 10–12

75 g (3 oz) fresh root ginger

1 tablespoon freshly ground black pepper

1 tablespoon fennel seeds, crushed

1 teaspoon dried chilli flakes

1 garlic clove, peeled and crushed

finely grated rind of 3 limes

50 g (2 oz) fresh coriander (cilantro),
    finely chopped

100 g (3½ oz) caster (superfine) sugar

75 g (3 oz) coarse sea salt

2 x 750 g (1 lb 10 oz) salmon fillets, skin on

salad leaves and thinly sliced grainy bread, to serve

FOR THE GARLIC SAUCE

200 g (7 oz) Greek (strained plain) yogurt

20 ml (4 teaspoons) lime juice

2 spring onions (scallions), finely chopped

1 garlic clove, peeled and crushed

Peel and finely grate (shred) the ginger into a bowl. Stir in the black pepper, fennel seeds, chilli flakes, garlic, lime zest, coriander, sugar and salt.

Check the salmon fillets and remove any stray bones. Place one fillet, skin side down in a large shallow, non-metallic dish. Spread the spice mixture onto the fillet in an even layer using the back of a spoon. Position the other fillet on top, flesh side down. Cover loosely with foil.

Place a dish containing kitchen weights or food cans on the fish to weight it down, then place in the refrigerator and chill for 2 days, turning the fillets twice daily, by which time the spice mixture will have turned to liquid.

To make the sauce, beat all the ingredients together in a bowl and transfer to a serving dish.

To serve, drain the fish from the liquid but don't scrape off the spices. Place on a board. Use a sharp knife to cut thin diagonal slices from the fillets similar in thickness to smoked salmon. Arrange on a bed of salad leaves and serve with the yogurt sauce.

fish escabeche with tomato and anise

᙭

An escabeche is an acidic marinade of Spanish origin that is used to semi-cure raw or lightly cooked fish. This marinade is a seasoned pickle that flavours and preserves the fish. Both oily and white fish work really well with this recipe.

Serves 4

8 herring or small mackerel fillets

30 ml (2 tablespoons) vegetable oil

½ red onion, finely chopped

15 ml (3 tablespoons) sun-dried tomato paste

4 whole star anise

100 ml (3 ½ fl oz) white wine vinegar

50 g (2 oz) caster (superfine) sugar

10 g (¼ oz) basil leaves, shredded

salt and freshly ground black pepper

rustic bread, to serve

Check the fish and remove any stray bones. Pat the fish dry on kitchen paper and season on both sides with salt and pepper.

Heat the oil in a frying pan over a medium heat and add the fillets. (You many need to cook them in two batches.) Cook gently for 1 minute then turn the fillets and cook for another minute. Transfer to a shallow non-metallic dish.

Add the onion, tomato paste, star anise, vinegar and sugar to the frying pan and bring just to the boil. Stir in the basil and pour the hot mixture over the fish so that each fillet is covered in a thin layer of the liquid. Cover loosely, allow to go cold and chill for 24 hours before serving. Use within 4 days, serving with chunky pieces of bread.

smoked mackerel, herb and garlic pâté

Nothing could be easier than blending some smoked mackerel with herbs and garlic to make a smooth, creamy textured pâté – completely failproof! It makes a simple fuss-free starter or snack, and keeps well in the refrigerator for a couple of days.

Serves 4

250 g (9 oz) smoked mackerel fillet

20 g (¾ oz) fresh coriander (cilantro), roughly chopped

20 g (¾ oz) fresh parsley, roughly chopped

30 ml (2 tablespoons) capers, rinsed and drained

1 garlic clove, peeled and chopped

45 ml (3 tablespoons) olive oil

10 ml (2 teaspoons) white wine vinegar

100 ml (3½ fl oz) sour cream

salt and freshly ground black pepper

Separate each mackerel fillet into chunky pieces, discarding the skin.

Put the coriander and parsley in a food processor with the capers, garlic, oil and white wine vinegar. Blend until the ingredients are finely chopped, scraping the larger pieces of herbs down from the side of the bowl with a spatula.

Add the fish to the processor and continue to blend to a thick paste. Add the sour cream and blend again until smooth and creamy. Season to taste with plenty of pepper and a little salt if needed.

Turn into a serving dish or individual dishes and cover loosely with cling film (plastic wrap). Chill until ready to serve.

smoked haddock and mushroom tart

❧

Smoked fish makes a tasty addition to pies. Here it is combined with flavourful mushrooms and a rich herby sauce. You could use ready-made shortcrust pastry if you are short on time, though the easy-blend recipe below is straightforward to make and has a lovely, buttery flakiness. Serve with a simple saad such as tomato and watercress.

Serves 6

175 g (6 oz) plain (all-purpose) flour
120 g (4 ½ oz) butter, chilled
1 egg yolk

FOR THE FILLING
600 g (1 lb 5 oz) undyed smoked haddock fillet
100 ml (3½ fl oz) milk
25 g (1 oz) butter
1 large onion, peeled and finely chopped

150 g (5 oz) chestnut mushrooms, thinly sliced
4 eggs
150 ml (¼ pint) single (light) cream
2 sprigs tarragon
freshly ground black pepper
50 g (2 oz) mature Cheddar or strong, hard cheese, grated (shredded)

To make the pastry, put the flour in a bowl and coarsely grate the butter into it. Stir frequently so that the butter doesn't stick together. Add the egg yolk and 45 ml (3 tablespoons) cold water. Mix into a dough using your hands, adding another up to 15 ml (1 tablespoon) of water if the dough feels dry. It should be firm, not crumbling apart. Turn out onto a lightly floured surface and knead into a ball. Wrap with cling film (plastic wrap) and chill for at least 30 minutes.

Preheat the oven to 200°C/400°F/Gas Mark 6. Thinly roll out the pastry on a lightly floured surface and use to line a 23 cm (9 in) diameter loose-base tart tin (pan) measuring 4 cm (1½ in) deep. Press the pastry firmly into the sides of the tin, moulding the pastry to seal any cracks. Trim the excess around the top of the tin. Line with greaseproof paper (baking parchment) and fill with baking beans. Bake for 20 minutes, then carefully lift out the paper and beans and return the case to the oven for another 5 minutes. Reduce the oven temperature to 180°C/350°F/Gas Mark 4.

To poach the fish, cut the smoked haddock into pieces to fit in a frying pan. Add the milk and bring to the boil. Cover with a lid, turn down the heat and cook gently for 5 minutes until the fish is opaque. There's no need to cook it through completely. Lift out the fish and set aside on a plate. Pour the liquid into a jug (pitcher). Wipe out the pan.

Melt the butter in the frying pan over medium heat and gently fry the onion for 5 minutes until softened. Add the mushrooms and cook for another 5–10 minutes, stirring frequently until the mushrooms are tender and any juices have evaporated. Tip into the pastry case.

Once the fish is cool enough to handle, break it up into large chunks, discarding the skin and removing any stray bones. Add the fish to the pastry case.

To make the sauce, whisk the eggs in a bowl and add the cream and fish cooking juices. Pull the tarragon leaves from the sprigs and add to the bowl with some pepper. Stir to combine. Pour over the filling and sprinkle with the cheese.

Bake for about 40 minutes or until golden and the centre of the tart feels lightly set.

salmon and dill tartare

There are two types of 'tartare' in culinary terms. The first is the familiar mayonnaise sauce flavoured with gherkins, capers and parsley, the second is the serving of raw fish, often referred to as 'tartare'. The simplest way of serving fish tartare is to pile the fish in the centre of a serving plate and surround it with the complementary ingredients so diners can blend and season to their own taste. In this recipe, the flavourings are mixed with the fish and moulded into little 'cakes'. It looks pretty and tastes lovely.

Serves 4

450 g (1 lb) salmon fillet, skinned and boned

4 spring onions (scallions), trimmed and finely chopped

4 tablespoons finely chopped fresh dill

1 tablespoon finely chopped fresh parsley

1 teaspoon salt

1 teaspoon caster (superfine) sugar

15 ml (1 tablespoon) grainy Dijon mustard

hard-boiled quail's eggs, halved, lime wedges and toasted grainy bread, to serve

Cut the fish into 5 mm (¼ in) thick slices. Pile a few slices together then cut into 5 mm (¼ in) thick strips, then cut across again to dice the fish. Transfer the fish to a bowl as you work.

Add the spring onions to the bowl with the herbs, salt, sugar and mustard. Mix well to ensure all the ingredients are thoroughly combined.

Place a 7 cm (2¾ in) metal ring on a baking parchment-lined tray or board and pack a quarter of the salmon mixture into it. Press down firmly with the back of a teaspoon then carefully lift away the ring. Mould three more in the same way. Chill until ready to serve.

Use a palette knife to transfer the cakes to serving plates. Surround with halved quail's eggs, lime wedges and toast to serve.

kedgeree with crushed spices

Kedgeree may be better known for serving at breakfast or as a brunch dish, but it's equally good for lunch or supper, particularly when you've added plenty of spices that give it a mildly curry-like flavour.

Serves 4

250 g (9 oz) basmati rice

4 medium eggs

700 g (1 lb 9 oz) undyed smoked haddock

100 ml (3½ fl oz) milk

10 cardamom pods

2 teaspoons fennel seeds

1 teaspoon cumin seeds

50 g (2 oz) butter

1 large onion, chopped

¼ teaspoon ground turmeric

50 g (2 oz) creamed coconut, finely grated

60 ml (4 tablespoons) finely chopped fresh parsley
   or chervil

salt and freshly ground black pepper

lemon or lime wedges, to serve

Cook the rice in plenty of lightly salted boiling water for about 10 minutes or until just tender. It should feel soft but retain a little bite. Drain well.

Put the eggs in a separate pan and cover with hot water. Bring to the boil, reduce the heat and simmer gently for 4 minutes. Drain and cool. Shell and quarter them.

To poach the fish, cut the haddock into pieces so that it fits in a single layer in a frying pan. Add the milk and cover with a lid. Cook gently for about 8 minutes, or until cooked through. Transfer the fish to a plate to cool, reserving any cooking liquid in a small bowl. Flake the fish into chunky pieces.

Crush the cardamom pods, fennel and cumin seeds with a pestle and mortar or put them in a small bowl and use the end of a rolling pin. If you like, take out the cardamom shells so you're only left with the tiny black seeds.

Clean the frying pan and melt half the butter. Gently fry the onion for 5 minutes until softened but not browned. Add the spices to the pan including the turmeric, the cooked rice, any reserved cooking juices, creamed coconut, parsley or chervil and fish. Gently stir the ingredients together. Add the eggs and season to taste. Heat through for a couple of minutes and serve hot with lemon or lime wedges.

potted salmon

'Potting' fish means encasing it in a buttery seal, which preserves it for several days, rather like a pâté. Lightly smoked salmon is great for this dish as it has plenty of flavour even when served cold, but is not as rich as traditionally smoked salmon. Serve with a well-flavoured bread such as a grainy oatmeal or rye.

Serves 6

200 g (7 oz) unsalted butter, diced, plus extra to grease

500 g (1¼ lb) lightly smoked salmon, skinned

¼ teaspoon ground mace

good pinch cayenne pepper

2 teaspoons lemon thyme, chopped

salt and freshly ground black pepper

Grease a large piece of kitchen foil with butter and arrange the salmon on the centre of it. Bring the edges of the foil up around the fish to enclose it, scrunching the foil together over the fish. (It doesn't matter if the top of the parcel is not tightly sealed.) Place in a frying pan or large pan containing a 1 cm (½ in) depth of boiling water. Cover with a lid and cook for about 20–25 minutes or until the fish is cooked through. Remove from the pan and leave to cool.

Put the butter in a small pan and heat gently until melted. Use a dessertspoon to skim off any foam that settles on the surface. Slowly pour the butter into a jug, leaving the white sediment that settles in the base of the pan.

When the fish is cool enough to handle flake it into very small pieces and put in a bowl with a generous half of the melted butter, the mace, cayenne pepper, lemon thyme, a little black pepper and salt, if necessary, to taste. Mix well and pack firmly into six small ramekin dishes, jars or other small serving dishes, each with a capacity of about 100 ml (3½ fl oz). Press down gently with the back of a dessertspoon.

Pour the remaining melted butter over the fish to seal it. Chill until the butter has set.

trout carpaccio

This raw fish dish requires the choicest, freshest fish available. Salmon or tuna can be substituted for the trout to give equally tasty results. Carpaccio' is the Italian term for very thinly sliced raw fish (or meat), sometimes lightly bathed in a dressing. This recipes incorporates the Japanese influence of serving raw fish by using sushi ginger and an Asian inspired dressing'. Serve as a stylish starter or snack, on its own, or with grainy bread.

Serves 6

300 g (10 oz) sea trout fillets

2 small celery sticks with leafy tips

15 g (½ oz) Japanese sushi ginger

small handful of mustard and cress

30 ml (2 tablespoons) mild olive oil

30 ml (2 tablespoons) mirin

15 ml (1 tablespoon) rice wine vinegar

1 teaspoon caster (superfine) sugar

Check the fish and remove any stray bones. Wrap the fish with cling film (plastic wrap) and freeze it for 20–30 minutes, so that the fish will be easier to slice thinly.

Place the fish on a board and cut into wafer-thin slices by making diagonal cuts down to the skin, then slice the fish so the skin can be discarded. Arrange the slices in a single layer on a large serving plate, or individual ones.

Roughly chop the leafy parts of the celery and slice the stalks as thinly as possible. Shred the ginger and mix with the celery, mustard and cress.

Whisk together the olive oil, mirin, rice wine vinegar and sugar. Drizzle over the fish. Scatter the celery mix over the fish and serve.

Basic recipes

fish stock

You can use almost any fish trimmings to make stock. The heads, tails, fins, skins and bones from white fish makes good stock but don't use oily fish, which can give a strong, greasy flavour. Prawn heads and shells can also be added.

Makes about 1 litre (1¾ pints)

25 g (1 oz) butter

1 onion, roughly chopped

2 carrots, roughly chopped

2 celery sticks, roughly chopped

1 garlic clove, peeled and sliced

1 kg (2¼ lb) white fish trimmings

small handful of parsley stalks

2 bay leaves

2 teaspoons black or white peppercorns

Melt the butter in a large pan and add the onion, carrots and celery. Fry gently for about 5 minutes until beginning to soften but not brown.

Add the garlic, fish trimmings, parsley, bay leaves and peppercorns, breaking the fish bones into pieces if necessary to fit in the pan. Add water until the contents are just covered – about 1.25 litres (2¼ pints). Bring to a gentle simmer and reduce the heat so the liquid is barely bubbling. As it cooks, skim off any scum that settles on the surface. (Don't let the stock boil or the flavour will spoil.) Cook for 30 minutes.

Remove from the heat and leave to stand for 15 minutes. Strain through a colander into a bowl. Store in the refrigerator for up to 2 days, or freeze in small quantities.

mayonnaise

Making homemade mayonnaise is a great culinary skill that's well within everyone's reach – and so impressive! It's great with grilled fish, fries and roasts, and with a few basic additions can be transformed into the quick and easy variations (see right-hand page).

Makes 300 ml (½ pint)

2 very fresh egg yolks

2.5 ml (½ teaspoon) Dijon mustard

salt and freshly ground black pepper

120 ml (4fl oz) mild olive oil

120 ml (4fl oz) vegetable oil

15–30 ml (1–2 tablespoons) white wine vinegar

Put the egg yolks, mustard and a little seasoning into a food processor or blender and blend briefly to mix.

Combine the oils in a jug (pitcher). With the machine running, gradually pour in the oil in as thin a stream as possible. The mayonnaise will gradually start to thicken. Continue adding the oil until the consistency is thick and smooth.

Blend in 15 ml (1 tablespoon) of the vinegar. Check the flavour, adding more vinegar for extra tang as well as a little extra seasoning as needed.

garlic mayonnaise

࿊

For a quick and easy version of a classic aioli, finely crush one peeled plump garlic clove and add with the egg yolks and mustard. Serve with fish stews, grills and barbecues.

saffron mayonnaise

࿊

On a chopping board, using a heavy knife and the heel of your hand, crush a peeled garlic clove and mix with a good pinch of saffron strands. Add a squeeze of lemon or lime juice and crush lightly again. Add to the mayonnaise with the egg yolks and mustard. Serve with fish stews, grilled, fried and barbecued fish, and braised dishes.

fresh tomato sauce

Ketchup might be good for everyday eating but this is better – fresh flavoured, tangy and sweet. If the tomatoes are slightly lacking in flavour add a couple of spoonfuls of sun-dried tomato paste. The sauce will keep in the refrigerator for a week or two and is great with fishcakes, oily fish, and chips, of course.

Serves 6

500 g (1 ¼ lb) ripe tomatoes

30 ml (2 tablespoons) olive oil

1 small onion, finely chopped

2 garlic cloves, crushed

15 ml (1 tablespoon) Worcestershire sauce

10 ml (2 teaspoons) Dijon mustard

1 teaspoon dried oregano

30 ml (2 tablespoons) light muscovado
(brown) sugar

salt and freshly ground black pepper

Pierce the skin of each tomato with a knife and place them in a heatproof bowl. Pour over boiling water and leave for 1 minute or until the skins split. Drain, rinse in cold water and peel away the skins. Roughly chop the flesh.

Heat the oil in a pan and gently fry the onion for 5 minutes or until softened. Add the garlic and fry for another minute. Tip in the tomatoes, Worcestershire sauce, mustard, oregano, sugar and a little seasoning. Cook gently for about 20 minutes, stirring the sauce frequently until it is thick and pulpy. Season to taste, and serve hot or cold.

hollandaise sauce

During the summer months, a beautiful piece of poached, grilled or barbecued fish needs nothing more than a delicious homemade Hollandaise sauce, some new potatoes and simply cooked seasonal vegetables.
Serves 4

30 ml (2 tablespoons) white wine vinegar

1 bay leaf

½ teaspoon black or white peppercorns

3 egg yolks

200 g (7 oz) unsalted butter, diced

squeeze of lemon juice

salt

Put the vinegar, bay leaf, peppercorns and 15 ml (1 tablespoon) water into a small pan and heat until bubbling. Keep a close eye on the pan and remove from the heat once the liquid has reduced to about 22.5 ml (1½ tablespoons). Strain into a food processor or blender and add the egg yolks.

Wash the pan and add the butter. Heat gently until melted. Use a spoon to skim off any foam that settles on the surface.

Start the machine running to lightly blend the egg yolks and vinegar. Continue blending, pouring in the butter in as fine a trickle as you can. The sauce will slowly start to thicken. Continue to add the butter.

Add a squeeze of lemon juice to give the sauce a slight tang. If the sauce is very thick, add a dash of hot water to thin it slightly. Season to taste and serve.

If the sauce curdles (as occasionally happens) pour it into a jug (pitcher). Clean out the processor or blender bowl and add 2 egg yolks. Slowly trickle in the curdled sauce until thickened and smooth.

samphire

Some fishmongers and supermarkets sell this delicious vegetable. Its natural salty sweetness and fresh crunchiness makes it a perfect accompaniment to fish dishes. Buy when you can as it's not available all year round.

Serves 4

200 g (7 oz) samphire

freshly ground black pepper

25 g (1 oz) butter, diced

Trim any coarse stem ends from the samphire and wash well in several changes of cold water to remove any grit.

Bring a pan of water to the boil, tip in the samphire and cook for 2 minutes. Drain thoroughly through a colander and return to the pan. Dot with butter and season with black pepper. Mix well and serve.

crushed minted peas

Complete the perfect fish and chip supper or grilled (broiled) fish dish with this chunky pea purée.
Serves 4

400 g (14 oz) fresh or frozen peas
small handful of fresh mint sprigs

30 ml (2 tablespoons) double (heavy) cream or
crème fraîche
salt and freshly ground black pepper

Cook the peas with the mint in boiling, lightly salted water until tender. Drain thoroughly, discarding the mint, and tip into a food processor.

Add the cream and a little seasoning. Blend, scraping the mixture down from the sides of the bowl. Keep it chunky or blend until completely smooth, whichever you prefer. (Alternatively mash the peas in the pan with the cream and seasoning until they're crushed but not puréed.)

chunky oven chips

ॐ

Ovencooked chips contain less fat than traditionally cooked chips, making them healthier. This method of cooking also means that once they're in the oven you can pretty much forget about them, apart from occasionally turning them so that they are evenly browned. And they taste good!

Serves 4

1 kg (2¼ lb) potatoes for chipping   salt and freshly ground black pepper

100 ml (3½ fl oz) mild olive or vegetable oil

Preheat the oven to 220°C/425°F/Gas Mark 7. Scrub the potatoes and cut into 1 cm (½ in) thick slices. Cut across in the opposite direction to make chips.

Brush a large roasting pan with a little of the oil and heat in the oven for 5 minutes. Add the potatoes and drizzle with the remaining oil, turning the potatoes until coated.

Bake for 45–55 minutes, turning the chips two or three times during cooking, until they're deep golden and crisp. Season with salt and pepper and serve.

About the author

Joanna Farrow is a food writer and stylist with thirty years experience, initially on women's magazines and then freelance, continuing to work for a variety of food and women's magazines. She has also written cookbooks on a diverse range of subjects including meat, fish, preserves, ice-cream, chocolate, baking and kids cooking. Since moving to a rural environment Joanna has developed a passion for gardening and has become thoroughly absorbed in her hugely satisfying herb garden. She also enjoys travelling and seeking out new culinary ideas to add a creative twist to recipe writing.

First published in 2012 by New Holland Publishers
London • Cape Town • Sydney • Auckland
www.newhollandpublishers.com

Garfield House	Wembley Square	Unit 1, 66 Gibbes Street	218 Lake Road
86–88 Edgware Road	Solan Street, Gardens	Chatswood	Northcote
London W2 2EA, UK	Cape Town 8000	New South Wales 2067	Auckland
	South Africa	Australia	New Zealand

10 9 8 7 6 5 4 3 2 1

ISBN 978 1 78009 001 6

Publisher: Clare Sayer
Publishing Director: Lliane Clarke
Project Editor: Simona Hill
Designer: Tracy Loughlin
Photographer: Graeme Gillies/NHIL/Myles New/Lis Parsons.
Stylist: Bhavani Konings
Home Economist: Jenny Fanshaw
Senior Production Coordinator: Marion Storz
Printed and bound in China by Toppan Leefung Printing Ltd

Picture credits: Alamy: p122–123. Corbis: p140, p200. Fotolia: p33, p146, p153, p156, p168, p175.
Shutterstock: p9, p11, p14, p65, p75, p202.